Hartmut Wilke

Turtles and Tortoises

Caring for Them
Feeding Them
Understanding Them

Photography: Uwe Anders
Illustrations: Renate Holzner

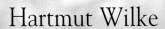

BARRON'S

CONTENTS

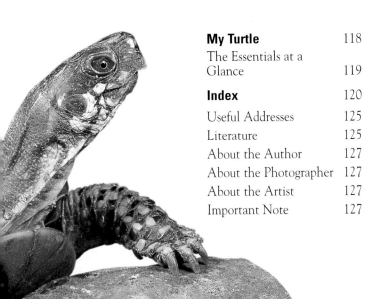

What You Need to Know Before Acquiring a Turtle

Turtles have lived on the earth for more than one million years. Retaining their primeval appearance, these witnesses to the past continue to fascinate humans.

Basic Information about Turtles

In the right environment and with proper care, a turtle can live for more than six decades, accompanying its owner from childhood into a ripe old age.

To enjoy your turtle for many years, you should be well informed about its needs and habits.

Habitat

Turtles need a warm environment and so are found primarily in the tropical and subtropical regions of the world. There are exceptions; a few species, such as the spotted turtle (see page 40), have been able to adapt to the seasonally changing climates of North America, Europe, and Australia. However, this adaptation was only possible because these species hibernate.

North and South America are home to a rich variety of turtles. These include many species of sliders and river cooters, such as the familiar red-eared slider (see page 39).

The musk turtle needs good footing for climbing, even under water.

In most of the United States, keeping a turtle in your garden pond is advisable only in the summer, from June to August.

Turtles live in a wide assortment of habitats. Sea turtles spend their entire lives in the ocean, and freshwater turtles live in large river systems and lakes; these aquatic turtles come ashore only to lay their eggs. Other turtles have found their way into rapidly flowing tropical mountain streams and have conquered steppes and deserts.

Turtles such as Horsfield's tortoise (see page 33) survive periods of heat and drought by burrowing into the earth and waiting in a state of limited activity, called *estivation.*

Some species of turtles, like sea turtles, are swift hunters; others, like the snapping turtles, are patient anglers or, like the matamata, lie in ambush and strike quickly when their prey comes within reach.

There are also turtles that live only in the water when

9

they are young, then spend extended periods on land when full-grown; an example is the Asian keeled boxed turtle, *Pyxidea mouhoti* (see page 46).

Natural History

As long as one million years ago, turtles shared the earth with dinosaurs and crocodiles. The turtles who lived then looked very much like the sea turtles of today.

A dandelion can tempt your tortoise to open its mouth so that you can easily look inside.

In Germany, fossilized turtles more than 20 inches (0.5 m) long have been found at the edge of the Harz Mountains. These are the oldest turtle fossils from the Mesozoic era to have been found so far.

These turtles had a long neck. Although the neck could not be withdrawn into the shell, it was protected by spiny protuberances.

The mouth of the fossilized turtles was found to contain small, knobby teeth, overgrown by the gums. Vestiges of teeth could also still be clearly identified on the jaws. This feature of their physical structure has since disappeared. Today's turtles have horny jaws with jagged edges.

The turtle's shell has also undergone a variety of adaptations during its evolution. An extreme example of this is the soft-shelled turtle, whose body is protected only by a tough, elastic skin. The former shell can now be seen only as a small patch on the underside.

Other species of turtles, such as the big-headed turtle, have a hard skull roof; as a result, it is no longer necessary or possible for them to retract the head into the shell for protection.

The very flat shell of the African pancake tortoise is reduced to a layer as thin and as resilient as a fingernail. To hide from its enemies, this tortoise squeezes into narrow cracks in its rock-strewn habitat.

The box turtle has joints and hinges in its shell. After pulling in its head, legs, and tail, this turtle can close its house up tight.

Sea turtles have a flat shell and a streamlined body, and their arms and legs have evolved into paddles. They can swim at speeds of more than 40 mph (70 km/hour).

The largest and heaviest of all turtles, the leatherback turtle, has only the vestige of a shell, in the form of seven bony ridges that support its leathery hide. Leatherback turtles can weigh as much as 450 pounds (about 200 kg).

Early Contact with Humans

The first encounters between humans and turtles probably ended less than happily for the turtles.

Exhibits in natural history museums bear witness to this.

In South Africa, turtle shells were coated with resin and wax and used as ornamental and functional containers. Decorated with cords, beads, and rings, such containers were used to store and transport dyes, medicinal herbs, or cosmetics.

Large turtle shells, like those of sea turtles, were used as serving bowls or as carrying containers for fruit and fish.

We do not know exactly why humans first began to hunt turtles. One reason was probably hunger, for turtle meat is tasty.

We know that early seafarers, whose journeys often lasted for months, relished this fresh meat. The sailors came ashore on the Seychelles or the Galapagos Islands, where they easily caught the giant turtles. They stored the turtles on their backs in the holds of the old sailing vessels, then killed them as they were needed for food.

In South America and Southeast Asia, freshwater

Turtles in History
Have turtles ever been worshiped by humans?

Yes, especially in regions where turtles lived. Humans in these areas considered turtles to be very special creatures. For example, more than 2,000 years ago, people believed that in the earliest beginnings, there was water everywhere. Then an immense turtle stood on the sea floor, so that its shell rose out of the water. On this hill, the world was formed. Some of the native peoples of North America also believed this. They thought turtles were friendly and clever animals. They even consulted them before making decisions. They would watch what a turtle did, then act accordingly.

In Asia, too, people had great reverence for turtles. They were especially fascinated by the different patterns on the turtles' shells. Fortune-tellers used these patterns to predict how long a man would live, for example, or whether a woman would have good luck or bad.

Turtle shells were also used to predict the future in Greece.

Earthworms and snails are among a three-toed box turtle's favorite foods.

turtles are still caught for food, and their eggs are harvested as well.

In Germany, the European turtle was a favorite food during Lent, when meat was not eaten. And it was barely ten years ago that true turtle soup (made from sea turtles) was considered a delicacy.

Some species of sea turtles have suffered because the large shields on their backs were used for the prized *tortoise shell*. Even until very recently, the tortoise shell was harvested by putting the living turtle, back first, into boiling water so the shell could be easily detached. Still alive, though scalped and scalded, the turtle was then thrown back into the sea.

However, there have always been people who were attracted to turtles just because they were interested in these creatures.

F. J. Obst, for example, describes a box turtle that was found in America in 1953. Carved into its *plastron* (lower shell) was the date 1844.

All over the world, serious turtle lovers, both hobbyists and professionals, are making efforts to ensure that turtles propagate even in captivity.

In the United States, three organizations, the National Turtle and Tortoise Society, the California Turtle and Tortoise Society and the New York Turtle and Tortoise Society work to promote captive husbandry techniques and breeding (see page 125). Museums and zoos have also contributed to positive developments with regard to the propagation of turtles.

Because of the research done on breeding, some species, such as the popular red-eared slider, can be bred in quantities on turtle farms.

Telling Turtles Apart

In the southern part of the United States, it is not at all uncommon to find a stray turtle in your yard, especially during the vacation months. The turtle may not have an owner; if you can't find out who owns it, and if you would like to keep the turtle, you'll need to determine whether you have a tortoise (living on land), a semiaquatic turtle, or an aquatic species (living mainly in the water). (We are assuming here that there is really no chance of your having a sea turtle wander though your yard.) The kind of turtle you have will make a great difference in its proper care and feeding.

By referring to the table on page 15, you should have no difficulty telling what kind of turtle you have found. There are some exceptions, of course. The shapes of the shells described in the table are for turtles that are at least two years old, with a shell at least three inches long (7–8 cm). Younger or smaller tortoises, for example, do not always have the distinctive high domed shell of a land turtle.

By referring to the table on page 15, you should

see page 125

TIP

To clear up any lingering doubt about whether you have found a tortoise, a freshwater turtle, or a semi-aquatic species, place the turtle in an enclosed area where there is both land and water, and watch it closely. To keep a land turtle from drowning, be sure the water has a gradually sloping bottom.

Young leopard tortoises are cute, but they can grow to almost 40 inches (70 cm) long!

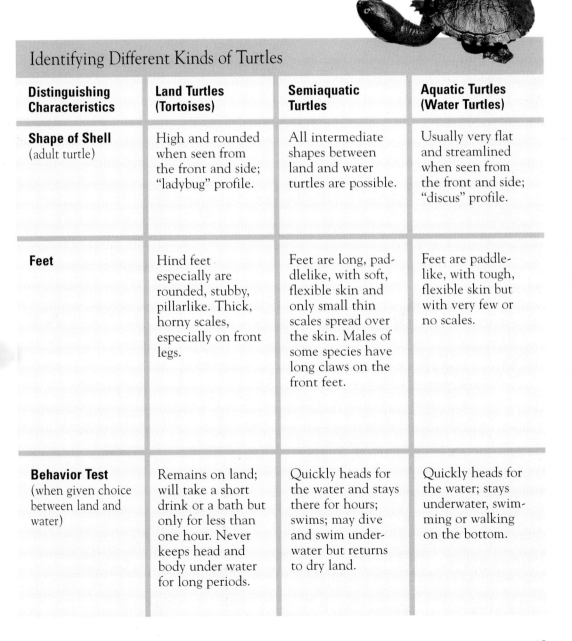

Identifying Different Kinds of Turtles

Distinguishing Characteristics	Land Turtles (Tortoises)	Semiaquatic Turtles	Aquatic Turtles (Water Turtles)
Shape of Shell (adult turtle)	High and rounded when seen from the front and side; "ladybug" profile.	All intermediate shapes between land and water turtles are possible.	Usually very flat and streamlined when seen from the front and side; "discus" profile.
Feet	Hind feet especially are rounded, stubby, pillarlike. Thick, horny scales, especially on front legs.	Feet are long, paddlelike, with soft, flexible skin and only small thin scales spread over the skin. Males of some species have long claws on the front feet.	Feet are paddlelike, with tough, flexible skin but with very few or no scales.
Behavior Test (when given choice between land and water)	Remains on land; will take a short drink or a bath but only for less than one hour. Never keeps head and body under water for long periods.	Quickly heads for the water and stays there for hours; swims; may dive and swim underwater but returns to dry land.	Quickly heads for the water; stays underwater, swimming or walking on the bottom.

15

Considerations Before Acquiring a Turtle

If your turtle is to stay healthy and contented, you must be ready to meet its needs. Listed below are some of the points you should certainly consider before acquiring a turtle.

Factors in Your Decision

1 Remember that a turtle can live to be more than 60 years old.

2 Many tortoises and freshwater turtles benefit from sunshine and fresh air. Can you set up a summer home for your turtle in your backyard, or in a garden pond, or on a porch or balcony? (see *"Favorite Kinds of Turtles,"* page 30).

3 The equipment needed to keep a turtle, especially an aquaterrarium for semiaquatic ones, is expensive.

4 Many species of turtles need to hibernate in winter, and some need a similar time of limited activity in summer, if they are to stay healthy (see page 30). This calls for extensive preparations on your part.

5 Keep in mind that the aquarium for an aquatic turtle is large and quite heavy. A medium-sized tank with 52 gallons (200 liters) of water, together with its stand and accessories, weighs about 550 pounds (250 kg).

6 Turtles are not cuddly pets. Many species are active during twilight and dark and spend the day in hiding.

7 It is not easy to give a turtle the varied diet it needs. Commercial turtle food must be supplemented with fresh food.

8 When you travel, you should leave your turtle at home. Do you have a reliable person to care for your turtle while you are away?

9 Because turtles are free from allergens, they make suitable pets for people who are allergic to animal hair.

10 Turtles do not carry parasites that can be transferred to humans. Almost all turtles carry salmonella bacteria, but transference can be avoided by simple hygiene techniques like never kissing a turtle (small children who are quick to

A mother tortoise and her
babies. Radiated tortoises
have been successfully bred
in captivity.

demonstrate affection will understand if you explain) and by washing your hands after handling your turtle.

One or Two?

Turtles are by nature solitary creatures, and they do not necessarily need a partner.

In the wild, turtles may be seen crowded thickly on the shore or basking on a sunny log. They do this, however, not from a need for company, but quite simply because space is limited. As soon as they have had their fill of sunshine, they go their separate ways.

During the mating season, they are more sociable for a time, but these are opportunistic pairings that do not last for long. One requirement for keeping a breeding pair is to be sure of the sex of your two turtles. You also need a terrarium of appropriate size, facilities to keep the two turtles separated when they are not getting along, a way to incubate the eggs, and a separate terrarium for raising the young.

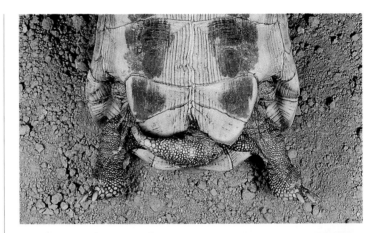

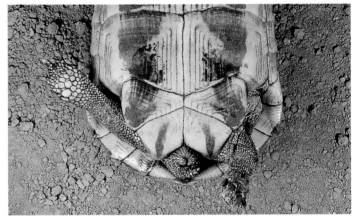

The Sexes

If you are looking for a suitable mate for your turtle, it is best to choose from nearly full-grown or adult turtles. The younger the turtle, the more difficult it is for someone who is not an expert to distin-

A male turtle's tail (top) is definitely longer than a female's (bottom).

guish between males and females.

In many species of turtles, the male's plastron is more concave than the female's.

Male turtles also usually have a somewhat longer tail, narrower at the base, with the vent closer to the end of the tail.

When in doubt, consult an experienced breeder.

Male painted turtles, even when half-grown, can be identified quite clearly by their front claws, which are obviously longer than those of females. These males are also already significantly smaller than the females.

In some species of turtles, the color of the eyes is another way to determine the turtle's sex (see pages 35 and 40).

A mature tortoise and a juvenile.

Surviving the Winter

For turtles in temperate climate zones, winter is a cold, hostile period when food is scarce; they survive only by hibernating.

In the wild, land turtles bury themselves under tree roots, in the dens of larger mammals, or in other places that are protected from the frost, not too wet and not too dry.

Freshwater turtles overwinter at the bottom of a pond, stream, or other body of water, where they burrow into the mud or under roots (see "Hibernation," page 65).

The best place for a pet land turtle to hibernate is an old-fashioned cellar with a hard dirt floor. This offers conditions like those found in nature: a relatively constant low temperature of between 32 and 50°F (0–12°C) and relatively high humidity.

A normal, unheated basement, where a window can be left open all winter, is also quite satisfactory.

If you don't have a space like this yourself, check with relatives, friends, or neighbors. Perhaps one of them will provide a spot for your turtle's hibernation box. Your local herpetological

19

Cuddly or Not?
Are turtles cuddly pets?

No, turtles do not like to be held and carried for very long. But if you enjoy watching animals, a pet turtle is just right for you. You will notice, for example, that turtles have a keen sense of smell. They will sniff closely at anything new. Turtles can also become quite tame. Feed your turtle often from your hand. Also, try rubbing the back of your turtle's head; many turtles seem to enjoy this. Your turtle may even learn to come when you call it.

society or one of the turtle or tortoise societies (for an address, see page 125) may also give you a list of contacts.

Inappropriate hibernation quarters for turtles include attics, backyard toolsheds, greenhouses, and balconies. Temperatures in such places fluctuate too widely in early spring and late fall, and if the winter is extremely cold, the turtle can freeze to death.

Note: If necessary, a small turtle can hibernate in the vegetable compartment of your refrigerator (see page 67).

Turtles and Other Pets

Never leave a turtle alone with another animal.

Dogs and cats include turtles among their natural prey. It is true that a dog can learn to respect a turtle as a companion. But if they are left unattended, an accidental rough encounter would surely be harder on the turtle than on the dog. Even with the best intentions, a dog who is trying to play with a turtle can injure it with his claws; this is especially true if the turtle is young and the dog is large. Likewise, something that looks like playful fun to a cat can mean danger to a turtle.

For healthy turtles, like this Hermann's tortoise, clambering over obstacles is good exercise.

Rodents such as mice, guinea pigs, or rabbits will not hesitate to try their teeth on a turtle. The outcome can be fatal, especially for small turtles.

Snake lovers should be aware that turtles carry pathogens that, although not harmful to humans, may cause diseases in snakes. For this reason, experienced reptile owners practice good reptile-keeping hygiene when keeping snakes and turtles in the same household.

Note: In an outdoor enclosure, whether in the yard or on the balcony, it is not unusual for a young turtle to be carried off by crows or magpies (see pages 62 and 63).

Children and Turtles

A school-age child can usually understand what a turtle needs and wants. However, parents must instruct their children appropriately. It is especially important to remind children that a turtle is a wild animal and will be shy of people, at least at first. If a child keeps touching the turtle, taking it out of the aquarium or terrarium, and carrying it around, the turtle will be alarmed and fearful.

Explain to your child that teaching a turtle not to be afraid of humans takes a great deal of patience and care. After a time, however, your turtle may become so tame that it will voluntarily come closer when you offer it a tidbit, such as a dandelion, in your outstretched hand. Even water turtles may willingly climb onto your hand once they are used to you.

Vacations

Turtles are happiest in their own familiar environment. You aren't doing your turtle a favor if you take it with you on your travels.

Plan ahead to find a reliable person to care for your turtle during your absence. The best caregiver is someone who is already familiar with turtles.

The checklist on page 23 will help you remember what you need to discuss with your turtle-sitter. In case of emergency, be sure to leave your vacation address and the name and address of your veterinarian. It's also a good idea to provide the telephone number of a person who knows about turtles and can give advice, if needed.

TIP

The age of a turtle can be determined with relative reliability only when the turtle is young. If you know the turtle's eventual adult size, and if your turtle is approximately one-third this large, it is about three years old. After another three years, it will have reached two-thirds of its adult size. You cannot tell a turtle's age by counting the growth rings on the plates of its shell.

Offered tasty dandelion greens, most tortoises will quickly become tame to your touch.

Checklist for Vacation Care

Equipment
- Explain how to tell if something is wrong. Demonstrate how to perform a simple inspection.
- Filter pump, timer, air pump if any: What if these are not working properly? Show what to do for simple repairs. If possible, provide the name and address of a knowledgeable person who can help.
- Explain procedures for routine care (such as cleaning filters).
- Have replacement light bulbs on hand. In the fuse box, identify the circuit breaker for the electrical equipment.
- If possible, have a spare pump on hand as well, or write down the model number, in case it is necessary to purchase a replacement, and where to purchase it.

Feeding
- Specify how much and what to feed.
- Specify how often and when to feed. (Have the person practice a few times while you watch.)

Turtle Care
- Describe normal behavior.
- Point out any peculiarities of behavior (see pages 30–47).
- Is it almost time for the turtle to hibernate or to lay eggs? (See pages 65 and 88.)
- Is the turtle just coming out of hibernation?
- Describe possible illnesses (see pages 81–85).
- Leave the address and telephone number of an expert who can be called on for advice.
- Leave your vacation address and the address of a suitable veterinarian.

Important: It's advisable for your turtle-sitter to learn about your turtle's particular habits and needs over the course of a year.

The Law and the Turtle Owner

Species Conservation

The Washington Convention on International Trade in Endangered Species of Wild Fauna and Flora (CITES) provides for the protection of flora and fauna whose worldwide survival is threatened. Depending on how much protection is needed, various species of turtles are listed in categories I or II. Animals threatened with extinction are listed in Appendix I. Other turtles are listed under CITES in Appendix II. Being placed on one of the CITIES appendices only means that special permits are needed before the animals can be imported into the United States; CITIES does not affect the sale or transport of animals within the United States.

Many states protect their native turtles and tortoises, forbidding harassment or removal from the wild and prohibiting private possession, commercial trade, or barter in the protected species. The Federal Endangered Species Act enforces state protection by prohibiting interstate transport, trade, or barter in any protected species. In addition, public health laws in the United States prohibit the sale or trade of any turtles under three inches in length, except for scientific purposes.

Be aware that individual states may change their regulations for individual species of turtles from time to time. Keep up to date on current regulations and laws by inquiring at your local state game and fish agency or at the game and fish agency of the state in question. It is your responsibility to check with the appropriate authorities to be sure your purchase is legal.

The Sales Agreement

Any well-run pet shop in the United States will provide the buyer with a detailed sales slip as a matter of course. This is only a receipt recording the financial transaction. It does not guarantee that you may return the turtle, even if it proves to be ill once you get it home. Before you buy the turtle, talk to the salesperson about the turtle's health, and ask about the store's policy on animal returns. If there is any doubt, ask if you can have your veterinarian check over the turtle within 48 hours of purchase, with a return for cash or credit possible if illness is found. (Be aware that turtles, like other reptiles, are slow to show illness; the result of a prolonged chilling or exposure to a toxic substance may not appear for a week or so, long after your agreement period has ended.) The store may choose *not* to permit the return of any livestock, for any reason.

The precautions may sound excessive; most pet stores take pride in selling healthy, feeding turtles with no health problems. But it is best to have an understanding reached before any problems arise.

Landlords and Turtles

Landlords are generally cautious about allowing

pets in their apartments. Your lease may specifically forbid you having a pet of any type, or it may forbid dogs, cats, or noisy birds such as parrots. Do not assume that your landlord won't mind if you bring in a few animals, even if the animals are just turtles. Ask when you rent your apartment, or ask before you buy and bring the turtles home. In the United States, breaking one of the rules within a lease agreement is considered breaking the lease, and legal action can follow; at the very least, your stay at the apartment may be uncomfortable and limited. Admittedly, turtles by their very nature are unlikely to cause a nuisance or make noise that could disturb other tenants. Furthermore, turtles can't cause serious damage to the dwelling, although the overflow from an unattended tank filling could damage the apartment below. Your landlord may ask for a modest damage

The black Caspian turtle lives in rivers and lakes.

deposit, but since he would rather keep a tenant than find a new one, negotiate!

Collecting Your Own Turtle

You may wish to collect your own turtle. Be certain you have permission before you venture onto private property, and do not collect turtles from state or federal lands (all animals and plants are protected on these lands). Find out which species are protected in the state where you are looking. Box turtles wander in the early morning hours, and aquatic turtles may venture onto roadsides in search of egg deposition areas. Driving in the early morning hours may be a good way to find a turtle, although "road cruising" for reptiles at night using lights is illegal in some states. Sunning aquatic

turtles may be netted off logs at the edges of ponds, but the approach must be by canoe to help cut off the escape.

Animal Rights

Turtles in the biotope of a terrarium are entitled to suitable living conditions. The physical surroundings in the terrarium, as well as the food, must be appropriate for the particular species. For water turtles, providing the proper environment includes changing the aquarium water regularly.

Tips on Buying a Turtle

Whether you buy your turtle, swap for it, or receive it as a gift, it is your responsibility to determine whether it is a protected species (see "Species Conservation," page 24). To do this, you need to know its scientific name. If you collect it yourself, be certain you know what you're collecting. If you buy the turtle, ask that the receipt state the Latin name of your turtle. This will be your written proof that you purchased what you thought was a legal species.

Where to Get a Turtle

A pet shop: You don't have to worry about buying a turtle from a pet shop. Your receipt, with the scientific name of the turtle, will serve as your turtle's "papers." However, you should be careful

about buying a species that is not protected. Never buy a turtle on the spur of the moment. Ask for the turtle's scientific name, and find out what sort of care it requires, before you buy. For example, the painted wood turtle, *Rhinoclemmys pulcherrima manni,* is often offered for sale. In Europe, these turtles are considered difficult to keep. In the United States, they are not only considered easy to keep but have been bred in captivity (see page 37).

Furthermore, many species become quite large; others, like the soft-shelled turtles and snapping turtles, though often sold in pairs, are

Hamilton's pond turtles bask on a sunny log.

At left: Horsfield's tortoise has a trim, athletic build.

suitable only for solitary living quarters.

A breeder: A breeder is a good place to look for an unusual species of turtle or tortoise. Breeders often advertise in magazines for terrarium and aquarium owners, as well as in the specialized turtle and tortoise publications. (see addresses, page 125).

It's best to visit the breeder to see how the tur-

tles are cared for, where they are kept, and what their winter quarters look like. You can also ask the breeder to show you his breeding stock for the species you're interested in; indeed, she may be able to show you your turtle's parents.

Note: If you can't find the turtle you want at a pet shop, you may be able to order one from a breeder. While you wait for your

27

turtle to be hatched, you'll have time to prepare suitable living quarters and learn how to take care of your future pet.

When to Get a Turtle

It's best to buy your turtle in the summertime—not earlier than May or later than September.

Buying in autumn a turtle that hibernates in winter can be very risky. It is often difficult for a lay person to determine whether an unresponsive turtle is about to hibernate or is ill. If you have actually purchased a sick turtle and keep it while it hibernates, it will most likely die before springtime.

It's also not advisable to buy a turtle that is just coming out of hibernation. If it had the beginnings of a health problem at the onset of winter, the problem will not become apparent for four to eight weeks after the turtle awakens.

Species from tropical regions do not hibernate. If you buy one of these turtles, however, you should keep in mind that they are very sensitive to drafts.

Tropical species must be kept absolutely warm and secure when they are moved in winter (see photos, pages 106–107).

Top: Test the shell of a young turtle with gentle pressure. It should be firm, but elastic.

Bottom: When held like this, a healthy turtle makes defensive motions.

Checklist for a Healthy Turtle

	Land Turtles (Tortoises)	Semiaquatic and Aquatic Turtles
Shell in good condition	*Young turtles*, up to one-third of adult size: Shell firm and elastic. *Adult turtles:* Shell hard and firm. All scutes (horny plates) firm and intact.	*Semiaquatic turtles:* As for land turtles. *Soft-shells:* Leathery shell, clean, no cracks, cuts, or open areas (inspect belly and edges).
Shell in poor condition	*Young turtles and adults:* Shell gives way when pressed, like crust on a dinner roll. *Adults:* Firm, but then changes shape. Individual plates very bumpy. *Plastron:* Holes in horny plate; pink, watery blisters.	*Semiaquatic turtles:* As for land turtles. *Soft-shells:* Leathery skin with white-rimmed, craterlike pits or spots; larger injuries partly white-rimmed; edges of shell may be damaged.
Skin healthy	Outside of heavy scales on neck and legs, skin is leathery, soft, and elastic.	*Semiaquatic turtles:* Leathery, soft, elastic. *Aquatic turtles:* Soft, elastic, smooth, intact.
Skin not healthy	Cracked? Ticks and mites?	Bloodshot spots or larger areas, with whitish fuzz (fungus).
Eyes healthy	Clear, bright, opened wide.	
Eyes not healthy	Cornea clouded, lids closed, swollen.	
Respiratory tract healthy	Dry when on land, no bubbles, no noise when breathing.	
Respiratory tract not healthy	Bubbles at nose and mouth, rattle when breathing.	As for land turtles. Also, may tilt on side when swimming.
Movement on land	All four legs used for forward motion; no dragging of rear legs (nerve damage).	
General responsiveness	When picked up, the turtle either moves vigorously in defense or pulls back strongly into its shell.	

Favorite Kinds
of Turtles

On the following pages are profiles of various turtle species that are often available in pet shops or from breeders.

What You Will Find in This Section

The profiles of tortoises or land turtles are given first, followed by accounts of semiaquatic turtles and aquatic turtles.

For each species, you will find information about their size, distribution, natural habitat, and behavior. Under "Care" are brief guidelines for tending that species of turtle. Recommended temperatures are given as a range; the upper limit should not be maintained all the time but, rather, should be reached only for about six hours during the daytime. Details about the equipment needed to house the various types of turtles are given on pages 50 through 63.

The feeding guidelines in each profile indicate only whether the turtle is carnivorous or herbivorous. Please also read the section on how to feed a turtle properly; it starts on page 70.

The information under *"Hibernation"* simply tells whether the turtle needs a period of relative inactivity in summer or winter. Further details about what you can expect and should provide are given in the section that starts on page 64.

Land Turtles (Tortoises)

HERMANN'S TORTOISE
(*Testudo hermanni*)

Size: Up to 8 inches.

Distribution: Greece and the Balkan countries, as far north as the Danube.

The subspecies *Testudo hermanni hermanni* is found in southern Italy. The subspecies *Testudo hermanni robertmertensi* is found in central and northern Italy; on the Balearic Islands, Corsica, and Sardinia; and in southern France and eastern Spain.

Habitat: Open, semiarid plains with scattered rocks and shrubs; abundant sun and partial shade. The tortoise hides in caves.

Behavior: Active by day, likes to climb and dig; very lively if given proper care.

Care: Terrarium and outdoor enclosure; average

Hermann's tortoise uses a birdbath as a watering hole, both for drinking and for washing.

temperature range 64°F at night to 79°F in the daytime. With no additional heat source, this tortoise can be kept outdoors in June, July, and August. With additional heat source, also May and September.

If daytime temperatures are cooler, an overhead spot lamp must be used to replace the sun's warmth.

In autumn and spring, before and after hibernating, this tortoise should be kept in a terrarium.

Diet: Leaves, grass, and other greens; in autumn, also hay (don't forget water!).

31

Hibernation: Yes, even during its first winter!

MEDITERRANEAN SPUR-THIGHED TORTOISE
(*Testudo graeca*)

Size: May exceed 12 in.

Distribution: Southern Europe, Iran, Egypt, Libya, Morocco. There are 4 subspecies; care is same for all.

Habitat: Open, semiarid and rocky plains. Hides in caves.

Behavior: Active by day, lively, likes to climb and dig.

Care: Terrarium and outdoor enclosure; air temperature 64°F at night to 79°F in the daytime. With no additional heat source, keep outdoors only from June to August; with additional heat source, also May and September. If daytime temperatures are cooler, use an overhead spot lamp. In autumn and spring, before and after hibernating, this tortoise should be kept in a terrarium.

Diet: Leaves, grass, and other greens, and in autumn, also hay.

Hibernation: Yes.

MARGINED SPUR-THIGHED TORTOISE
(*Testudo marginata*)

Size: About 12 inches.

Distribution: Southern Greece; also has been introduced into Sardinia.

Left, an adult Mediterranean spur-thighed tortoise; right, a margined spur-thighed tortoise.

A margined spur-thighed tortoise is happy in summertime on warm soil with scattered vegetation.

Horsfield's tortoise digs tunnels that can be as long as 12 yards (almost 12 meters).

Hibernation: Yes.

Special notes: Hermann's tortoise and margined tortoises can interbreed. For species protection, such crossbreeding should be avoided.

HORSFIELD'S TORTOISE
(*Testudo horsfieldii*)

Size: Up to 8 inches.

Distribution: East of the Caspian Sea, in deserts and mountains from Iran to Pakistan.

Habitat: Open, karstic (limestone) regions with dry, sandy, and loamy soil. Hides in caves.

Care: Terrarium and outdoor enclosure; air temperature 64°F at night to 79°F in the daytime. With no additional heat source, keep outdoors from June to August; with additional heat source, also May and September. If daytime tem-

Habitat: Sunny slopes with grass and shrubs.

Behavior: Active by day, likes to climb and dig.

Care: Terrarium and outdoor enclosure; air temperature 64°F at night to 79°F in the daytime. With no additional heat source, keep outdoors from June to August; with additional heat source, also May and September. On cold days, use an overhead spot lamp. In autumn and spring, keep in a terrarium.

Diet: Leaves, grass, and other greens; in autumn, also hay.

peratures are cooler, use an overhead spot lamp. In autumn and spring, keep in a terrarium.

Behavior: Active by day, likes to climb and dig.

Diet: Leaves, grass, and other greens; in autumn, also hay.

Hibernation: Yes.

Special note: May have a period of limited activity in summer (4–5weeks).

BELL'S HINGED-BACKED TORTOISE

(*Kinixys belliana*)

Size: 8 inches.

Distribution: Central and southern Africa, Madagascar.

Habitat: Plains, with dry, sandy to gravelly soil.

Behavior: Active by day.

Care: Terrarium and outdoor enclosure; air temperature 68°F at night to 86°F in the daytime. Outdoor enclosure only in good

weather, from June to August.

Diet: Grasses, other greens, and fruit.

Hibernation: No (but there are exceptions).

Special note: Carapace is jointed, allowing tail end of the shell to close.

HOME'S HINGED-BACKED TORTOISE

(*Kinixys homeana*)

Size: 8 inches.

Distribution: West Africa.

Bell's hinge-backed tortoise lives on the plains of Africa.

Home's hinge-backed tortoise enjoys the soft, moist, warm soil of the tropical forest floor.

Most male ornate box turtles have glowing red eyes.

Habitat: Tropical rain forest with soil rich in leaves and humus.

Behavior: Active by day.

Care: Terrarium with tropical atmosphere (humidity above 70 percent), air temperature 75°F at night to 86°F in the daytime.

Note: Do not let the soil get moldy. The air must always smell fresh and tangy. Provide good ventilation and a moist corner.

Diet: Grasses, greens, and fruit.

Hibernation: No.

Special note: Carapace is jointed, allowing tail end of shell to close.

ORNATE BOX TURTLE
(*Terrapene ornata*)

Size: Up to 6 inches.

Distribution: U.S., between the western tributaries of the Mississippi.

Habitat: Grassland; sandy, semidry soil with low bushes, near bodies of water. Hides in caves.

Behavior: Crepuscular (active in morning and evening twilight). Stays in caves during the day.

Care: Terrarium and outdoor enclosure; air temperature 64°F at night to 82°F in the daytime. May be kept outdoors from June to August. In autumn and spring, keep in a terrarium. Box turtles like early morning and late afternoon sun.

Diet: Hunts down and devours grasshoppers, crickets, and locusts. Some specimens may eat greens and mushrooms. Others in Europe have eaten poisonous mushrooms without getting sick.

Hibernation: Yes, even in the first winter.

Special notes: Hinged plastron allows this turtle to close itself almost completely in its shell. The sexes can be distinguished by the color of the eyes. In all box turtles, the iris in the male is reddish brown to orange in color—the iris in the female is yellowish white to yellow. These turtles don't do well in captivity, especially in areas of ground fog or high humidity. Only those experienced in turtle care should attempt to keep box turtles as pets.

Crosses between various species of box turtles are possible, but should be avoided for the sake of species protection.

RED-FOOTED TORTOISE
(*Geochelone carbonaria*)
Size: Up to 20 inches.
Distribution: Tropical South America.
Habitat: Rain forest with soil rich in leaves and humus.
Behavior: Active by day.
Care: Terrarium with humidity above 70%, air temperature 75°F at night to 86°F in the daytime.
Note: Do not let the soil get moldy. The air must smell fresh and tangy. Provide good ventilation and a moist corner hideaway.
Diet: Grasses, greens, and fruit.
Hibernation: No.

SERRATED HINGE-BACKED TORTOISE
(*Kinixys erosa*)
Size: Up to 12 inches.
Distribution: West Africa.
Habitat: Tropical rain forest with soil rich in humus.

Top: A healthy red-footed tortoise displays brilliant colors.

Bottom: The serrated hinge-backed tortoise, *Kinixys erosa,* has a hinged carapace, allowing the tail end of the shell to close.

requires good ventilation and a moist corner.

Diet: Grasses, greens, and fruit.

Hibernation: No.

Freshwater Turtles

The following species are often considered to be land turtles, because they spend more time on land than other semiaquatic species:

- Painted wood turtle (*Rhinoclemys pulcherrima manni*). There are other subspecies as well.
- *Pyxidea mouhoti*, the Asian keeled box turtle
- *Heosemys* species from Asia. *Heosemys spinifera* tends to be more aquatic than *Heosemys* species.

Painted wood turtles are often sold in pet shops, and most will do well in the United States. They feed on earthworms, dry dog kibble, and fruit.

Shelter: Aquaterrarium with one-third water and two-thirds land; water temperature 80°F; air temperature 80–82°F. An overhead spot lamp in one corner of the terrarium provides a warm spot with a temperature of 97°F. The aquaterrarium should be covered

Top: Caring for a Central American wood turtle can be very challenging.

Bottom: The twist-necked turtle's aggression towards others makes it a difficult species to keep in captivity.

Behavior: Active by day.

Care: Terrarium with humidity above 70%, air temperature 75°F at night to 86°F in the daytime.

Note: Do not let the soil get moldy. The air must smell fresh and tangy. This and the humidity must be kept at 85–95%. It is essential to ensure that there is no decay, in the form of rot or mildew.

Note: Some of these turtles are described in greater detail in the profiles of aquatic turtles below (see pages 46–47).

COMMON MUSK TURTLE (STINKPOT)

(*Sternotherus odoratus*)

Size: Up to 6 inches.

Distribution: U.S. (Florida) to southern Canada.

Habitat: Still waters, abundant vegetation.

Behavior: Active day and night; hearty eater; poor swimmer.

Care: Aquaterrarium and garden pond; provide water temperature of 68 to 77°F for specimens from the northern U.S., 73 to 82°F for those from the southern U.S. Air temperature 75 to 82°F. May be kept in a garden pond from June to August, or May to September for northern species.

Diet: Carnivorous.

Hibernation: Depends on place of origin.

Special notes: Place roots, stones, or even sisal rope ends (2½ inches in diameter) in the terrarium to help the turtle climb around. In garden pond, be sure the shore is gently sloping. These turtles secrete a foul-smelling

The musk turtle can't swim very well. Even in water, it needs good footing.

The North American wood turtle comes from the northern United States and feels comfortable in the latitudes of central Europe as well.

Always on the alert! When danger approaches, the red-eared slider disappears underwater in a flash.

substance called *musk* when disturbed.

NORTH AMERICAN WOOD TURTLE
(*Clemmys insculpta*)

Size: Male 5 inches, female up to 9 inches.

Distribution: U.S. and Canada, from Great Lakes region to Nova Scotia.

Habitat: Largely terrestrial; margins of cool rivers and streams, marshes and bogs.

Care: Terrarium, or outdoor enclosure with hut shelter; air temperature should be 65 to 80°F. May be kept outdoors from April to October with no hut shelter; from early March to late October with heated shelter.

Behavior: Active by day; can climb over wire-netting fence 6 feet high. Bend the top 4 inches over to prevent climbing. Intelligent; enjoys being outdoors.

Diet: Snails, worms, beetles, berries, and fruit.

Hibernation: Yes. Hibernates under water or burrows under the soil on land. Provide a cool aquaterrarium and let your turtle choose where to overwinter.

Special notes: Protected from capture or harassment in the U.S. Only captive born babies can be legally sold. May exhibit violent mating behavior and aggression; best for experienced turtle fanciers.

Species requiring similar conditions:

■ Blanding's turtle, *Emydoidea blandingii*, size up to 5 in. for males, up to 11 in. for females. In shallow ponds and marshes with decayed bottom, in northern and north central U.S. Relatively shy. Largely protected in the U.S. throughout its range.

RED-EARED SLIDER
(*Trachemys scripta elegans*)

Size: Up to 10 inches.

Distribution: Southern U.S., east and west of the Mississippi. Has been very successfully introduced in the Pacific Northwest and New England.

Habitat: Still waters with abundant vegetation.

Care: Aquarium and garden pond; in aquarium, water temperature 79 to 82°F, air temperature 79 to 90°F. May be kept in a garden pond from June to August. In the remaining months, except when hibernating, keep in terrarium.

Behavior: Active by day; enjoys a sunny resting place close above the water; lively swimmer.

Diet: Juveniles carnivorous, adults also herbivorous.

Hibernation: Yes, in the first winter as well. Never leave them in the garden pond for the winter!

Species requiring similar conditions:

■ Cumberland slider, *Trachemys troosti*, to 10 in. long.

■ Hieroglyphic river cooter, *Pseudemys concinna hieroglyphica*, 16 inches long.

■ Twist-necked turtle (*Platemys platycephala*), 6 to 7 inches. This edge dweller follows high water into the forest and may be stranded as the waters recede. Once on land, it may burrow to await rising waters.

SPOTTED TURTLE
(*Clemmys guttata*)

Size: Up to 5 inches.

Distribution: Eastern and northeastern U.S.

Habitat: Small, marshy meadow ponds and slow rivers.

Behavior: Active by day, when the water is warm enough. Often lives sub-

A spotted turtle looks for food—perhaps a tasty snail?

Top photo: Reeves' turtle has three distinctive keels along its carapace.

Bottom photo: A yellow-bellied slider.

merged; likes to bask in the sun when the water is cold.

Care: Aquarium and outdoor enclosure; water temperature 72 to 81°F, air temperature 72 to 82°F. May enjoy a garden pond

from June to August, but only on hot sunny days; its body temperature must reach 97°F.

Diet: Carnivorous.

Hibernation: Yes.

Special notes: Males have brown eyes, females yellow. Length of hibernation depends on place of origin. Watch its behavior when hibernating.

Best kept in spacious quarters or as a solitary pet because even a pair may not get along if their quarters are cramped.

REEVES' TURTLE

(*Chinemys reevesii*)

Size: Up to 7 inches.

Distribution: Indonesia, Japan, southeastern China.

Habitat: Calm fresh and brackish bodies of water.

Behavior: Active by day.

Care: Aquarium and garden pond; provide an easy way to climb out of the water because this turtle is a poor swimmer. Garden pond from June to August but only on hot days when the water temperature reaches 80°F. Air temperature 75–82°F.

Diet: Carnivorous.

Hibernation: No.

41

MISSISSIPPI MAP TURTLE
(*Psuedogeographica kohnii*)

Size: Up to 10 inches.

Distribution: Southern United States.

Habitat: A riverine species; may be found in oxbow ponds with abundant vegetation and plentiful insects and fish.

Behavior: Active by day.

Care: Aquarium with an island for sunning; place in garden pond only on hot summer days. The turtle must be able to maintain a body temperature of 97°F in the sun. Water temperature 72 to 82°F, air temperature 72 to 82°F.

Note: Turtle must have an island where it can dry off and sun itself.

Diet: Chiefly insectivorous/carnivorous; may eat a little vegetation. Likes snails, mollusks, worms, crustaceans, and insects.

Hibernation: Determine the need for hibernation by observation.

Species requiring similar conditions:

■ Black Caspian turtle, *Mauremys caspica leprosa*. Size, up to 10 inches. Lives in the rivers of Spain, Portugal, and Algeria.

■ False map turtle, *Graptemys pseudogeographica* Size, up to 10 inches. Four subspecies; inhabits fertile waters of the United States. Chiefly insectivorous. Determine the need for hibernation by observation.

Top photo: The yellow-margined box turtle requires the same care as the Malayan box turtle.

Bottom photo: Slow and steady: the black marsh turtle.

A Malayan box turtle heads to the surface for a breath of fresh air.

■ Caspian turtle, *Mauremys caspica caspica*. Size, up to 10 in. Found in slowly flowing rivers south of the Caspian Sea; three subspecies. Chiefly herbivorous, with 30–50% meat. Determine the need for hibernation by observation.

MALAYAN BOX TURTLE
(*Cuora amboinensis*)

Size: Up to 8 inches.

Distribution: Southeast Asia.

Habitat: Shallow lakes and ponds with shallow shores. These turtles also spend time on land.

Behavior: Active by day. Poor swimmer.

Care: Aquaterrarium with underwater climbing aids such as rocks, roots, or sisal rope ends so the turtle can easily reach the surface of the water. The land portion should be 30 to 40 percent of the total area. Water temperature 75 to 86°F, air temperature 79 to 86°F.

Note: If the temperature drops below 64°F for even a short time, the turtle will become chilled and will develop a respiratory infection!

Diet: Omnivorous.

Hibernation: No.

Species requiring similar conditions:

■ Yellow-margined box turtle, *Cuora flavomarginata* (see photo, top of page 42). These turtles are found in the Philippines and in Sulawesi; some specimens may be wholly terrestrial.

BLACK MARSH TURTLE
(*Siebenrockiella crassicollis*)

Size: Up to 8 inches.

Distribution: Southeast Asia, tropical rain forest and savanna.

Habitat: Ponds, streams, rivers.

Behavior: Active by day; calm temperament.

Care: Aquarium with underwater climbing aids (roots, stones, etc.) Water temperature and air temperature 75 to 86°F.

Diet: Omnivorous (half meat).

Hibernation: No.

SPINY SOFT-SHELL
(*Trionyx spiniferus*)
(See photo, page 44.)

There are 23 species of *Trionyx* worldwide. The most commonly encountered are the species from the U.S. (*Trionyx ferox, trionyx spiniferus*).

Size: Male 6 inches, female up to 18 inches.

Be careful about species and place of origin. African soft-shelled turtles can grow to 24 inches, and they can deliver a painful bite.

Distribution: Primarily central and eastern U.S.

Habitat: Marshy rivers, streams, and lakes.

Behavior: Active by day.

Care: Aquarium; also in garden pond from June to August. Water temperature 72–81°F, air temperature corresponding to water temperature. Use fine sand in the bottom of the aquarium (river sand, never sharp-grained, or use plastic pellets). Provide an island (see page 55) for sunning.

Diet: Meat (also water snails).

The shell of the spiny soft-shelled turtle has evolved to just a leathery jacket.

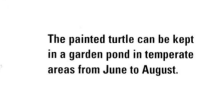

The painted turtle can be kept in a garden pond in temperate areas from June to August.

A pair of Australian snake-necked turtles mating. In water, the webbed feet are clearly evident.

Photo at right: The baby snake-necked turtle hatches after three months.

Hibernation: Depends on origin, and can be determined only by observation.

Note: Keep alone. The shell is very sensitive, prone to fungus, and injuries heal poorly. The water *must* be clean. A bite from an adult soft-shell can cost a finger.

PAINTED TURTLE
(*Chrysemis picta*)
Size: Up to 10 inches .
Distribution: U.S., east of the Mississippi, and in the north west of the Mississippi.
Habitat: Calm waters, rich in vegetation.

Behavior: Active by day; fairly constant alternation between sunning and foraging.
Care: Aquarium and garden pond; water temperature 68 to 77°F, air temperature 68 to 77°F. In aquarium, provide an overhead spot lamp above an island for warming. Keep in garden pond from June to August.
Diet: Omnivorous (half meat).
Hibernation: Most need hibernation, but some examples from the southern part of the range do not.

COMMON SNAKE-NECKED TURTLE
(*Chelodina longicollis*)
Size: Up to 12 inches.
Distribution: Eastern Australia.
Habitat: Still and slowly flowing water, shallow shore. In rainy season, also temporarily on land.

Behavior: Active by day, lively swimmer, likely to bite during mating period.

Care: Especially spacious aquarium; water temperature 73 to 82°F, air temperature 75 to 82°F.

Diet: Carnivorous; likes fish and earthworms.

Hibernation: No.

Special notes: This turtle, a member of the sideneck family, turns its head and neck and tucks it under its carapace for protection.

EASTERN MUD TURTLE
(*Kinostermon subrubum*)

Size: Up to 5 inches.

Distribution: United States, plains of the Mississippi and its tributaries, east coast.

Habitat: Still, shallow waters, rich in vegetation, with gently sloping banks.

Behavior: Active at dawn and dusk. Poor swimmer, spends lots of time on land. Aggressive against other turtles and members of the same species; beginners should start with a single turtle.

Care: Aquaterrarium and garden pond. Fill half the aquaterrarium with a land section, the other half

with water with a gently sloping bottom for easy exit. The turtle can live in the garden pond from the end of May to September. Water temperature 73 to 75°F, air temperature 72 to 82°F.

Diet: Primarily carnivorous. Offer young turtles 50 percent water insects and 50 percent soft greens (pond plants, soaked lettuce) Offer older turtles meat and some plants.

Hibernation: Depends on place of origin. Determine need for hibernation according to behavior.

Special notes: Two transverse hinges permit the

The keeled box turtle, *Pyxidea mouhoti,* is primarily aquatic when young, and later chiefly terrestrial.

Top photo: The Vietnamese leaf turtle likes fast-flowing waters.

Bottom photo: The big-headed turtle is aquatic for its entire life.

plastron to close the shell opening.

These turtles can give off a strong-smelling secretion. Adult males can be distinguished from females by their highly cornified, spiny-tipped tail.

KEELED BOX TURTLE
(*Pyxidea mouhoti*)

Size: Up to 7 inches.

Distribution: Vietnam, Laos.

Habitat: In and around waters of the tropical rain forest.

Behavior: Juveniles are primarily aquatic, while older turtles are chiefly terrestrial. They burrow in the moist, leafy forest floor and enjoy the green shade.

Care: Aquaterrarium; water temperature 73 to 77°F, air temperature 73 to 77°F, soil temperature 68 to 72°F.

Diet: Omnivorous.

Hibernation: No.

Special note: This species of turtle has a pronounced hook on its upper jaw, which it uses in climbing. This hook must not be removed. Provide an overhang for the outdoor pond enclosure fence.

When the turtle is nearing adulthood, a transverse joint develops in the rear third of the plastron.

Species requiring similar conditions:
■ Asian leaf turtle, *Cyclemys dentata.*

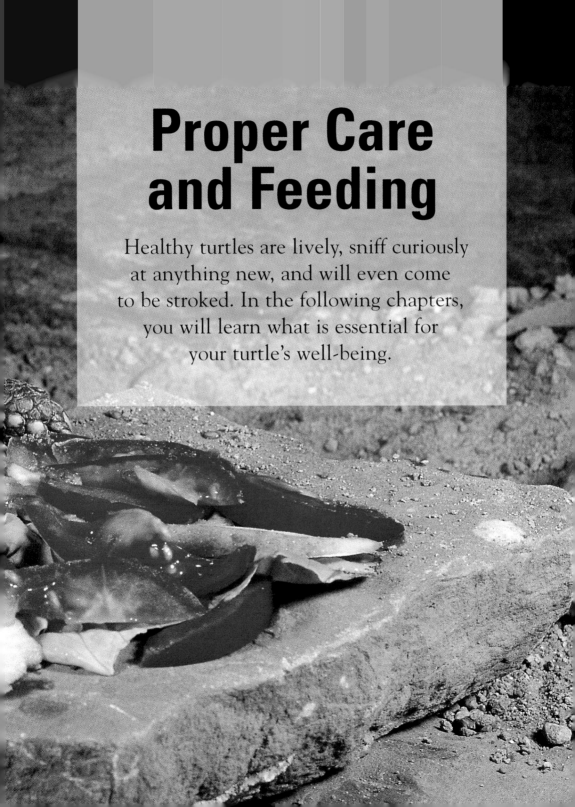

Proper Care and Feeding

Healthy turtles are lively, sniff curiously at anything new, and will even come to be stroked. In the following chapters, you will learn what is essential for your turtle's well-being.

What a Turtle Needs

The most important requirement for keeping your turtle happy and healthy is an appropriate shelter with the right equipment.

Indoors

TERRARIUM FOR LAND TURTLES

A well-equipped terrarium for tortoises must provide the following (see drawing, page 52):

■ a place to hide away at night;

■ a bathing pool with warm water (72–75°F, 22–24°C);

■ a warm area of sand or stone (75–79°F, 24–26°C in the daytime);

■ a sandy area at room temperature (64–72°F, 18–22°C);

■ a corner with moist, unheated sand.

Warmth is provided by electrically heated rocks (available at pet shops). All you have to do is plug them in. Be sure to cover the electric cord with a flat rock so the turtle can't dig it up and chew on it!

Other ways to provide the necessary warmth:

■ First place a sheet of pressed cork, ½–1 inch (1–2 cm) thick, on the floor of the terrarium to cover ½–⅓ of its area.

TIP

Here's how to calculate the minimum dimensions for a terrarium for a tortoise: Multiply the length of the adult turtle's shell by 5 (for example, 8 inches × 5 equals 40 inches; 20 cm × 5 equals 100 cm). The base of the terrarium should then be 40 inches by 40 inches (100 cm × 100 cm = 1 m²), or about 10 square feet, for each turtle of this size.

A dead tree limb is great for climbing.

How to Care for Different Kinds of Turtles

	Shelter	Care of Shelter	Feeding	Most Common Errors in Care
Land Turtle (Tortoise)	Terrarium (dry); also outdoor enclosure; possibly hibernation box. Enclosure is simple; technical equipment needed (see page 50).	Simple.	Chiefly herbivorous; on land.	Keeping turtle on the floor leads to eye and lung inflammations.
Semiaquatic Turtle	Terrarium with pool (aquaterrarium); also outdoor enclosure with pond; enclosure more complicated; technical equipment needed (see page 53).	Simple, but change water often.	Chiefly carnivorous; in water and on land.	Inadequate hygiene leads to infections (eyes, skin, intestines, plastron).
Aquatic Turtle	Aquarium; also outdoor enclosure with pond; hibernates in aquarium; technical equipment needed (see page 55).	More work because large volume of water needs to be changed.	Chiefly carnivorous; in water.	Drafts and water that's too cold leads to eye and lung inflammations.

This will be the base of the heated area.

■ On top of this, place three layers of aluminum foil, shiny side up.

■ On the aluminum foil, place an electric heating mat with a thermostat (available at pet shops), about the same size as the foil area. The heating mat will also heat the water basin from below.

To set up the terrarium:

■ Place a floor tile of fired clay (terra-cotta) on the heating mat.

■ Next to this tile, set a water basin made of clay, porcelain, or metal. A good choice is a shallow rectangular clay flowerpot large enough to accommodate an adult turtle comfortably. The edge must be low so even small turtles can get in and out without difficulty.

Note: Young turtles can drown in the water basin. For them, the water should not be any deeper than the middle of the shell!

■ Now cover the terrarium floor with a half-and-half mixture of fine-grained, washed river sand and bark chips.

■ Arrange roots and rocks

Terrarium for land turtles. The glass lid protects against drafts, but it should cover only two-thirds of the top. The overhead spot lamp provides the necessary warmth, and the ultraviolet lamp ensures healthy bone growth for your turtle.

A stepping stone gives young turtles safe footing.

Stepping stones also help semiaquatic turtles climb in and out of deeper pools.

Terrarium with large bathing pool, for a semiaquatic turtle. The glass cover slides back and forth to allow adjustments of temperature and humidity.

in such a way that the turtle must climb over or around them. Also give your turtle a place to hide.

■ An overhead spot lamp (60–100 watts) provides artificial sunshine. It's important for the turtle to be able to warm itself under the lamp to temperatures above 86°F (30°C).

If the terrarium is located in a relatively dark spot, connect the lamp to an electric timer. Set the timer to provide daylight hours appropriate for the season.

■ Plants are not essential, but they look pretty in the terrarium.

If the terrarium is in a dark spot, you will need to install a special plant lamp (available in florist or pet shops) to keep the plants healthy. Choose sturdy plants, such as *Aechmea* or *Schefflera*. It's best to set the plants in clay pots and cover their soil with rocks or roots to protect them from being nibbled.

TERRARIUM FOR SEMI-AQUATIC TURTLES

Semiaquatic turtles appreciate a land area with interesting variety and a pool of water for swimming and diving (see drawing, bottom of page 52). It's important to know what your particular turtle requires (see pages 30–47). A good swimmer needs plenty of room to swim. A turtle that climbs around under water must have objects to provide good footing (see drawing, bottom of page 52). For a semiaquatic turtle that spends most of its time on land, the land area must take up at least half the space.

The terrarium should definitely be watertight; it's a good idea to buy an aquarium right from the start.

The terrarium size for a single semiaquatic turtle can be calculated as indicated for a land turtle in the tip on page 50.

To set up the terrarium, start with the directions for the land area of a terrarium for tortoises (beginning on page 50). For a semiaquatic turtle, however, the following guidelines also apply:

■ It's best to use two thermostat-controlled floor heating units, one for the water area and one for the land area. A heating stone (see page 50) is an option for the land area. Temperatures in the enclosure should be between 77 and 85°F (25–29°C), and 95°F (35°C) under the heat lamp.

■ Fill the land area with a mixture of sand and bark chips, as described on pages 52 and 53.

■ Place flat rocks around the edge of the pool, to help keep the water clean. These rocks can also be heated from below to provide a basking spot.

■ Depending on your turtle's needs, the water area should take up one-third to one-half of the total space. Construct the pool so that the turtle can glide slowly into the water (see drawing, page 53). At its deepest point, the water should be a little deeper than the width of the turtle's shell. Otherwise, if the turtle falls on its back, it may be unable to right itself in the shallow water, and it can drown.

A large, deep clay bowl makes an excellent pool for semiaquatic turtles.

■ An overhead spot lamp

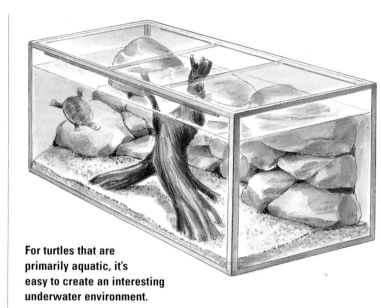

For turtles that are primarily aquatic, it's easy to create an interesting underwater environment.

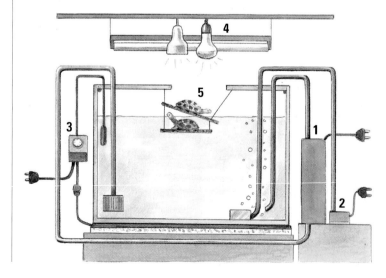

(60–100 watts) serves as a heat source.

■ Plants inside the terrarium will soon be eaten. It's best to place decorative marsh plants around the outside.

AQUARIUM FOR AQUATIC TURTLES

First, determine whether your aquatic turtle is a good swimmer or a less enthusiastic one (see pages 37–47).

Energetic swimmers want as much swimming space as possible. For that reason, not only the surface area, but also the depth of the aquarium is important.

The minimum size for the aquarium is calculated as follows: The length should equal five times the shell length of the adult turtle. The width is three times the shell length. A 5-inch turtle will need at least a 15-gallon aquarium.

This calculation does not include any space for decorations. Therefore, increase the calculated aquarium volume by about 30 percent. Add another 30 percent if you want to keep two turtles in the same aquarium.

Setting up the aquarium is a simple matter if you are content with the minimum of equipment (see drawings, pages 54 and 55).

■ Cover the glass bottom with a thin layer of washed sand, so it won't act as a mirror.

■ A piece of ridge tile on the aquarium floor, large enough so the turtle doesn't get trapped, provides a hiding place; a branch of resinous wood from a bog gives the turtle something to climb on underwater and serves as a basking surface above-water.

■ Gather flat stones and build a wall at the rear of the aquarium to provide an attractive setting. This also gives poor swimmers a way to clamber out of the water. Polyurethane foam glue or ready-mix cement helps keep the stones in place. Leave a narrow space of about 1–2 inches (3–5 cm) between the stones and the rear wall. This will later allow you to insert a tube to suction out the dirt that settles there. It works best to place a Styrofoam block against the rear of the aquarium before you build

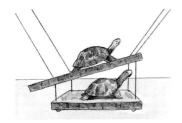

A sunning island on the top level, with a hiding place below.

Equipment for a water turtle's aquarium: Filter with integrated heating element and pump (1); aerator (2); and heating element with timer (3), only if not included in (1); lighting (4); and island for basking (5).

the stone wall, then remove it when the wall is complete.

Caution: Young turtles must be kept out of this crevice. They could get stuck there and drown. Close the gap with a strip of Styrofoam (remove it for cleaning).

■ The most convenient way to simultaneously heat and filter the aquarium water is to use a pump-driven filter that contains a thermostat-controlled heating unit (available in pet shops). Separate filtering and heating units are also available. When choosing a filter, consider whether your turtle prefers calm or flowing water (see pages 37–47). This will determine the necessary pump output. The more

Horsfield's tortoises can dig long tunnels for shelter in hot summers.

T I P
▼

Use this rule of thumb to select the proper pump for a turtle that likes flowing water: The pump should be capable of circulating the aquarium water in 10 to 15 minutes. The lower the pump's location, the higher

A flowerpot saucer is big enough for this small tortoise to wash in.

water the pump puts out per minute, the stronger the water flow and turbulence in the aquarium.

Note: Aeration of the aquarium water is not needed if the water is already being circulated by a filter pump. However, a ventilator stone set in the base can help to keep decaying matter circulating, so it can be filtered out.

■ Freshwater turtles like a place just below and at the surface of the water, where they can rest and sun themselves. Take two pieces of cork board about one-half inch (1 cm) thick, and glue each one to a piece of plexiglass with epoxy glue. Fasten the two together at all four corners with very strong wire to make a two-story structure (see drawing, page 55). The wire must

be stiff, so the island won't wobble. Suspend the structure from the edge or a crosspiece of the aquarium frame.

The lower level should rest horizontally under the surface, just deep enough so the turtle can crane its neck and breathe. The upper level, set off to one side if possible, should be slanted so the turtle can easily crawl up onto it.

■ A glass lid or closed cover protects against drafts. It should be installed in such a way that there is an opening in the middle, above the sunning island.

■ Hang an overhead spot lamp and a full spectrum light (Vita-Lite by Duro-Test) over this opening. Read all labels and ask your pet store for help in buying full-spectrum lights; in the United States, bulbs claiming to be full spectrum may actually be only color corrected.

WHERE TO PUT THE TERRARIUM OR AQUARIUM

The ideal location is under a glass roof, such as in a greenhouse. Here the

A birdbath makes an ideal bathtub for this Hermann's tortoise.

turtle experiences the changing day lengths of the different seasons. This has an important influence on its readiness for hibernation (see page 65) or breeding (see page 86). Rooms with large windows are also very suitable.

Undesirable is a room without daylight, unless adequate artificial light is provided.

Be careful of drafts. They are harmful for all turtles. Equally dangerous is placing a terrarium or aquarium directly by a window. In winter, the window gets so cold that cold air drops downward. This constant flow of cold air makes the turtle sick. Never let your turtle crawl about on the floor, unless you provide a sheltered area with a heat lamp. Even in rooms with heated floors, air circulation causes a draft.

Note: Take care not to allow vibrations from a refrigerator, stereo equipment, the aquarium pump, or the like to be transferred to your terrarium or aquarium. Turtles are easily disturbed by such vibrations.

QUARANTINE IS IMPORTANT!

Before placing a newly acquired turtle in its own terrarium or aquarium, or together with others of its kind, you should first put it in quarantine. Otherwise, there is too great a risk that it will carry diseases or introduce harmful bacteria or parasites into the main terrarium or aquarium (see page 78).

A quarantine terrarium can be improvised in a plastic mortar pan (from the hardware store) with a capacity of 12–65 gallons (50–250 liters).

For tortoises, all that's needed is newspaper lining the bottom, a hiding place, such as a board resting on two bricks, and a dish for food and water.

For semiaquatic turtles, the quarantine terrarium can be equally spartan, but these turtles also need a bathing pool of appropriate size.

Note: A 60-watt light bulb suspended just above the terrarium can serve as an improvised heat source for the quarantine period.

Keep the temperature at 77–85°F (25–29°C).

For aquatic turtles, set a piece of ridge tile down to provide a hiding place, then add water until the top of the tile just forms an island protruding from the water. Of course, the necessary filters and pumps must be connected to the quarantine aquarium (see page 55).

Outdoors

OUTDOOR ENCLOSURES FOR TORTOISES

If turtles don't get enough light, sunshine, and vitamins, they can develop *rachitis* (rickets). In that case, the shell will be deformed. A good way to prevent this is to keep the turtle outdoors from June to August. If you provide a cold frame with an additional heat source (see page 61), you can put the turtle outdoors in May and leave it out through September (see drawing, below).

Size of outdoor enclosure: It should be at least four feet wide and 10 feet long (1.2 × 3 m).

Fencing: Set cement slabs, lawn-edging tiles, smooth wooden planks, or corrugated plastic (available from garden shops) in the ground. Take care that the turtle can't reach the

A dream vacation for tortoises—June to August in an outdoor enclosure.

top edge of the enclosure with its front feet, or it will climb out.

Ground: Excavate to a depth of about 1 foot (30 cm); the ground must have a grade of about 2 inches per yard (5 cm per meter). Leave mounds and hillocks that protect the turtle from high waters and serve as a basking spot.

Vegetation: Sow grass and weeds (dandelions, chickweed) and plant low shrubs (box). Rocks and roots may be used for decoration, but they should not permit the turtle to climb out.

Cold frame: At the upper end of the enclosure, in a sunny spot, install a cold frame made of plexiglass as a shelter. Because of the greenhouse effect, this will hold sufficient warmth even in relatively long periods of bad weather. For a doorway, you can easily cut a rounded opening in the plexiglass with a fretsaw.

Note: Cold frame kits can be purchased in garden shops. A glazier will have to cut the plexiglass pieces. These are easily inserted into the frame kit.

It's best to make the floor of the shelter from cement slabs (they store heat well).

Heat source: For cold days, when the temperature in the hut doesn't reach 79°F (26°C), install an

The outdoor pen for semiaquatic turtles provides natural living conditions.

infrared lamp or a 60–80-watt light bulb, that can hang from the ceiling.

Feeding spot: A stone slab in front of the cold frame serves as a dining area and makes it easier to clean up food remnants from the pen. The stone slab should be in the shade, so that fresh food doesn't wilt too quickly in the sun.

Bathing spot: At the low end of the pen, install a shallow pool with a drainage ditch to allow rainwater to run off. A birdbath (made of cement or plastic, sold in garden or pet shops) makes a suitable pool.

As in the terrarium, so here too, the rule is that the turtle must be able to crane its neck and breathe comfortably from the deepest spot of the pool. The pool should also contain rocks or roots to help a turtle that's lying on its back to right itself.

Cover: Turtles less than 4 inches (10 cm) long are easy prey for crows, magpies, or cats.

A cover made of wire mesh or netting will protect the turtle.

ENCLOSURES FOR AQUATIC TURTLES

Many aquatic turtles can be kept in a garden pond from June to August. The pond should hold at least 80 gallons of water. For pools from this size to about 50 cubic feet, a ready-made garden pond can be purchased. A ready-made pond should be installed at a slight angle. At the lower edge, excess water can then run off in the right direction (provide drainage ditches if necessary). For larger ponds, you might also consider a plastic liner (see drawing, page 61). For climbing and sunning, a thick log can be placed in the pond so the turtle(s) can climb onto it.

Vegetation: the most suitable choices are reeds and cattails. Anything else will be eaten, as will small fish, newts, and insect larvae.

Filtering: Pools with a capacity of up to 50 cubic feet must be filtered; filtering is optional for larger ponds. Install a simple submersible pump at the bottom of the pool and an external pool filter nearby (both are available in garden and pet shops).

Fresh summer air on the balcony. Left, for a tortoise; right, for a semiaquatic turtle.

Storm hooks and rubber cords secure the cover of a balcony enclosure against severe storms.

Fencing: Planks, planed smooth and treated with a preservative, or lawn-edging tiles made of concrete, metal, or corrugated plastic (found in garden shops).

A fence that rises 1½–2 feet high and extends about 1 foot into the ground will suffice. A 4-inch overhang will keep climbing turtles inside the enclosure.

Cover: To protect small turtles from cats, crows, or magpies, and from gulls if you are near the seacoast, cover the enclosure with bird netting or a fishnet.

A Minipond on the Balcony or Patio

An attractive outdoor enclosure for water turtles can be constructed on a balcony or patio (see drawings at left).

■ Build a box from squared timbers and spruce boards, about 5–6 feet long, 2 feet wide, and 2½–3 feet high. To keep the box from rotting, line it with a plastic sheet fastened at the edges with waterproof adhesive.

■ For a cover, use two plexiglass panes screwed to a frame made of roofing laths. Have the cover extend a little over the front edge (for rain protection). The box should be about 4–6 inches lower in front than in back so the plexiglass panes lie at an angle. This allows more sunlight to enter, and the rain can run off better.

■ For a pool, depending on the number of turtles, use one or two mortar pans from a hardware store or a ready-made pool.

■ Fill the bottom of the box 8–12 inches deep with sand or light expanded clay aggregate (from a garden shop). Or you can also use sand.

■ Place the pool on the layer of aggregate. Be sure the top of the pool is at least 12 inches below the edge of the box so the turtle can't climb out.

■ Fill the box with garden soil to the edge of the pool.

■ Add plants and decorations to your landscape to suit your own taste.

■ Line your balcony with mesh so any escaped turtles or tortoises cannot fall off.

Note: For tortoises, a birdbath can be substituted for the pool.

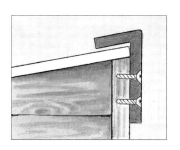

At the back edge of the cover, attach a metal angle as reinforcement.

Proper Care for a Healthy Turtle

Turtle care includes not only cosmetic measures, such as trimming overgrown claws, but also preparing the turtle for hibernation. Naturally, it's also very important for your turtle's health to keep the equipment in the terrarium or aquarium working properly.

Grooming

Claws will grow too long if your turtle walks around too little or the ground underfoot is too soft. The claws will not wear down as they should. For tortoises, too much animal protein in the feed leads to excessive claw growth and doming of the scutes on the carapace.

The long claws hinder the turtle's movement and must be trimmed with special clippers (see drawing, page 66). These are sold in medical supply stores. It's best to have your veterinarian teach you how to trim the claws.

Note: The males of some freshwater turtles, such as

The radiated tortoise willingly stretches out its neck to be stroked.

Outdoors, ticks can lodge in folds in the turtle's skin. These parasites can be removed easily with special tick pullers purchased from outdoor suppliers or some drug stores.

Tweezers are useful for removing splinters or bits of loose skin.

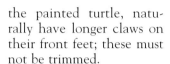

Have the veterinarian show you how to trim your turtle's claws with special clippers.

the painted turtle, naturally have longer claws on their front feet; these must not be trimmed.

The horny beak around the mouth may grow to be too long if the turtle's food is too soft. In tortoises, too much protein in the diet can also cause this. The horny excess must be filed off by a veterinarian (see drawing, page 66). Preventive measures include giving harder food and offering cuttlebone or limestone to gnaw on.

Note: The painted wood turtle, for example, naturally has a hook on its upper jaw, which aids it in climbing. This must never be trimmed.

The shell actually needs no cosmetic care; however, you may rub a very small amount of petroleum jelly into the shell every three or four months. Then carefully rub the shell dry with a soft cloth.

Hibernation

Many species of turtles need a period of relative inactivity in winter, even in captivity. Observe your turtle's behavior to determine whether it is ready to hibernate. In October, as the length of the day and the strength of the sun decrease, both terrestrial and aquatic turtles become more sluggish. They have little appetite or stop eating altogether.

Note: Turtles from temperate and semitropical areas need to hibernate even during their first year of life. However, you should weigh your hibernating turtle every five to six weeks. If its weight decreases by more than 10 percent from one weighing to the next, your turtle is sick and must be awakened prematurely.

ESTIVATION

The Horsfield's tortoise undergoes a period of relative inactivity during especially dry and hot summers in its native habitat (see page 33). When kept outdoors as a pet, it may also sense this need. Its behavior will resemble that of a turtle before hibernation.

HIBERNATION FOR TORTOISES

Before it goes into hibernation, the tortoise must be

bathed every day for a week in warm water (75–79°F, 24–26°C) for 10 to 20 minutes so it can completely empty its bowels. During this period, do not feed it at all. Then turn off the heat and light in the terrarium for two to three days.

The room temperature should also be below 64°F (18°C). When the turtle shows the behavior described on page 65, place it in its hibernation box.

The hibernation box measures 28 × 28 inches (70 × 70 cm) and is 32 inches (80 cm) high (see drawing, page 67). It is made of boards loosely fastened together, so that air can penetrate into the box. Fill the bottom of the box to a depth of about 4–8 inches (10–20 cm) with moist lava rock or clay aggregate (from a garden shop). Next comes a 4-inch (10-cm) layer of moist garden soil. Finally, fill the box to about 4 inches (10 cm) below the edge with peat moss and leaves, dry but not too dry. Place the turtle on this layer. It will dig its own way into the lower layers. Finally, cover the box with

cheesecloth or wire mesh. The room temperature can vary between 32°F and 54°F (0–12°C), but it must not be above 54°F (12°C) for more than one week or else the turtle will awaken too soon.

Note: While it hibernates, the turtle must not be fed. It will not disturb the turtle to weigh it. Take care that the layers in the box do not become too dry. Moisture protects the turtle against dehydration. If necessary, add a small amount of water in a corner at the level of the garden soil.

The turtle will wake up after three to five months. Take it out of its hibernation box and place it in its shelter in a quarantine terrarium (see page 58). Set the terrarium in a relatively warm room (68–72°F, 20–22°C) and wait until the turtle comes out of hiding. Bathe it in warm water (75–79°F, 24–26°C), give it a drink, and place it in its terrarium.

HIBERNATION FOR FRESHWATER TURTLES

In the wild, most freshwater turtles overwinter in the muddy bottom of a

Special clippers for trimming claws that have grown too long.

Parasites are removed with special tick pullers.

A veterinarian needs to file down this beak.

Hibernation box for a tortoise. Bottom layer, lava cinders or clay aggregate; middle layer, garden soil; top layer, peat moss and leaves.

Freshwater turtles overwinter comfortably in a layer of foam pellets and shallow water.

pond, river, or other body of water (see pages 30–47). Freshwater turtles from tropical areas, such as *Platemys*, do not hibernate.

Winter quarters can best be established in a black plastic mortar pan (see page 58).

Shelter for a smaller turtle can be provided by a ridge tile; for larger turtles, create a cave effect by covering most of the pan with a board to block out light.

The water level should be shallow enough that a turtle sitting on the bottom can breathe by craning its neck.

The water temperature can vary between 34°F and 54°F (1–12°C), but it should not stay above 54°F

(12°C) for long, or the turtle will awaken too soon.

Change the water every three to four weeks. Change the water immediately if it turns yellowish or if a whitish film forms on the water.

Note: Aeration and filtering are not necessary in the hibernation quarters. The turtle must not be fed while it is hibernating.

A *refrigerator* can provide emergency hibernation quarters for your freshwater turtle if a suitable cellar location is not available. Cover the glass plate above the vegetable bin with foil to block the light. The vegetable bin itself serves as the hibernation container; set it up like the mortar pan arrangement described on this page. You may omit the ridge tile.

Note: See if your turtle will accept an artificial mud bottom. Cut a piece of plastic foam in chunks and fill the bottom of the mortar pan or vegetable bin with a loose layer of these. This gives the turtle the feeling of being dug in.

Warning: Be very careful about hibernating species

from semitropical areas outdoors in northern garden ponds. The winters are too long, and the risk of harming the turtle's health is immense.

Bring your freshwater turtle out of hibernation after 75 to 100 days maximum by moving the pan to a warm room [72°F, (22°C)] and waiting until the water has reached room temperature.

Put the turtle back in the aquaterrarium or aquarium, with water at the same temperature. Turn on the heating and lighting systems again. After another five to seven days, the turtle will resume its normal level of activity.

Equipment Maintenance

Electrical cords: If exposed to excessive heat, the cords of lamps can become brittle or start to melt. Replace as necessary (observe safety precautions

A turtle's eardrum is located behind the area of dark skin below the eyes.

Hibernation
Does a hibernating turtle need to be fed?

Many land and water turtles become very slow in October. They go into a state of rest, resembling sleep, that lasts for more than four months. In the wild, they do this to survive the harsh winter. Food is scarce in winter, and a turtle's body does not stay warm in cold weather. Land turtles often bury themselves under tree roots for the winter. Water turtles burrow into the muddy bottom of the pond or river where they live. Turtles do not eat or drink during their winter rest. They live on energy stored up from the food they ate from spring to fall. But this does not mean that they will starve. Their hearts beat very slowly while they are asleep, they do not breathe as fast as usual, and they move hardly at all. As a result, they use very little energy. Their reserves are enough to keep them alive. You must not feed your pet turtle while it is hibernating; a healthy turtle does not need it. However, if a young turtle loses a great deal of weight during its winter rest, you should wake it up and take it to the veterinarian to see if it is healthy.

when handling electrical cords).

Filter pump and filter housing: Hard water can cause mineral deposits; use an appropriate commercial product to remove these. Most grocery stores or hardware stores sell products to remove lime deposits. Hoses and tubes can be removed and placed in a bucket with a formic acid solution to remove deposits.

The pumps in modern aquarium filters are generally maintenance free. On the other hand, it is important to keep the pump's water intake clean. If the water is very dirty, silt can accumulate here and clog the turbine bearing. For this reason, silt deposits should be removed regularly.

Fittings: Hose connections and the like can loosen over time. Check them regularly.

Air pump: Dirty filters should be replaced; reusable plastic filters may be washed in warm water, dried, and reinstalled.

A Varied Diet Is Important

The best way to prevent disease is to give your turtle a varied diet of healthy foods. Turtles easily become partial to a particular food. You must keep in mind that feeding your turtle the same thing all the time can lead to health problems.

Plants in the Diet

Mother Nature sets an abundant table for tortoises. Grasses, weeds, and bushes offer a wide variety of leaves, blossoms, and fruits. On the plants are insects, caterpillars, and snails, which meet the tortoise's very slight need for animal protein.

To feed your pet turtle, it's best to forage for greens in your yard or garden. Choose dandelions or daisies, chickweed, clover, grass (in autumn, also hay, always served with a drink of water), tops and tubers or roots of carrots, kohlrabi, and other vegetables. Lettuce and other leafy vegetables grown outdoors are also a good idea.

Caution: Avoid greens and vegetables that have been sprayed with weed killers or pesticides. Don't feed your turtle poisonous plants.

A varied diet is important but not always easy to maintain. Turtles tend to prefer their favorite foods and spurn the other healthy choices you offer. You can outwit your pet turtle by mincing the other foods and mixing them into the food it likes best.

Meat in the Diet

Freshwater turtles are omnivores; they eat both plants and animals. In general, however, they prefer meat. Many species (such as the red-eared slider) switch over; they are entirely carnivorous as juveniles and gradually increase the amount of plants in their diet as they grow.

Suitable dietary staples for these turtles include fat-free ground beef, small aquarium fish (guppies or bait minnows), or bits of filleted freshwater fish, such as trout. Frozen fish must be thawed and brought to the water temperature of the aquarium before it is given to the turtle. To keep a steady supply of fresh meat

Weigh your turtle once a month to determine whether it is growing properly.

Flowers, like this hibiscus blossom, add variety to a tortoise's diet.

on hand, you can breed water snails in a small aquarium (your local pet store can get you started).

If you are away from home for a long time, your turtle-sitter will find it convenient to feed your turtle dry cat food. It is economical and contains calcium, vitamins, and minerals—exactly what a freshwater turtle needs. Unfortu- nately, the dry food pellets also contain fats that are difficult to digest; there- fore, while this can be a basic food, it should never be given as the only food your turtle gets.

Note: If the dry food causes diarrhea, stop giving it until your turtle's diges- tive system returns to nor- mal. Then give it in smaller amounts.

Dietary Supplements

Calcium, vitamins, and trace elements (available in pet shops or from a veterinarian) are essential for a turtle's healthy development.

Vitamins and trace elements are provided in commercial diet supplements, such as ReptaMin® or Osteoform®. These are generally sold as powders. Every turtle, small or large, needs one pinch of this powder twice a week. Mix it thoroughly with your turtle's favorite food.

Note: If a turtle is eating fresh ground beef or fish, or while it is kept outdoors in the summer months, vitamin supplements are usually not needed. Too many vitamins can even cause health problems. For example, an excess of vitamin A in tortoises can cause an inflammatory skin disease that can be fatal (see page 84).

Aquatic turtles, on the other hand, are more likely to suffer a vitamin A deficiency, which causes swollen eyelids, especially in young turtles (see page 83). Because the body can produce vitamin A, it

should only be necessary to provide the materials it needs to do so in the form of foods high in carotene. Pet shops offer special fish food called Koi-Chow, which also gives the turtle's skin a splendid color and makes the yellow or red spots and stripes stand out beautifully.

Calcium is important especially for shell development in growing turtles and for formation of the eggshells in adult females. Calcium is available as a special preparation in pet shops, or you can meet your turtle's needs by adding ground eggshells to the diet. Until your turtle is two years old, sprinkle calcium over its food daily; later, twice a week will suffice.

Note: Bananas, tomatoes, and peaches are high in phosphorus. The balance of calcium to phosphorous in a turtle's diet must be 2:1. When you offer phosphorous-rich foods, offer calcium-rich foods such as broccoli or supplements the next day. It's preferable to sprinkle calcium for tortoises on

At right: A mortar and pestle make it easier to grind up eggshells.

Washed and ground eggshells help prevent calcium deficiency.

Standard Foods for Different Seasons

Season	Land Turtles	Freshwater Turtles
Basic Diet		
Spring	Greens: chickweed, dandelions, daisies, plantain, grass, fresh tree leaves.	Fresh trout (bring frozen pieces to water temperature before feeding), fat-free ground beef, dry cat food (no more than 50 percent of total food).
Summer	See Spring.	See Spring.
Autumn to winter (do not feed during hibernation.)	Romaine lettuce, kohlrabi leaves, leafy hay.	See Spring.

Feed foods fresh or prepared as an aspic (see page 75).

Year-round	Dietary supplements: Twice weekly, one pinch of a mineral/vitamin mixture (ReptaMin® or Osteoform®; see page 72); at every meal, calcium (ground eggshells), grated carrots or Koi-Chow (available at pet shops).

Note: This table gives recommendations for your turtle's basic diet. Please also observe the special notes regarding nutrition in the profiles on pages 30 through 47.

greens and romaine lettuce. For freshwater turtles, knead diet supplements into a small amount of ground beef.

The Right Amount

Unfortunately, there is no hard and fast rule about how much a turtle should eat. However, a healthy turtle often eats more than is good for it. Resist your turtle's begging. Too much food will cause obesity, liver damage, or infertility.

Tortoises eat slowly, making it difficult to estimate

the right amount of food. Over time, you must develop a feeling for how much food your tortoise needs.

If the folds of its skin bulge out of its shell when it draws in its legs, you should put your tortoise on a diet. Reduce the amount of food by about 30 to 40 percent, until the fat deposits under its skin are no longer in evidence.

Note: Tortoises are always fed on dry land. Be sure that fresh drinking water is always available.

For water turtles, the right amount to feed can be determined as follows: First, let the turtle go without food for a day. Then choose its favorite food. Weigh the food you are going to give or measure it by level teaspoons. Feed the turtle until its first eagerness subsides and it obviously starts to eat more slowly or selectively. Now weigh or measure the amount of food remaining, and subtract this from the initial amount. Divide the difference by two. The result will give you an approximate idea of how much to feed your turtle.

Note: Water turtles should always be fed in the water. If two turtles of different size are kept together, the larger one may bite off the smaller turtle's head if they are both trying to eat the same morsel. For this reason, young turtles should always be fed separately from adults.

Make Your Own Turtle Food

The recipe below comes from the kitchen of the Frankfurt Zoo. This complete turtle food can also be made in bulk and frozen in portions for later use.

■ Food for herbivorous turtles:

Eighty-five to ninety percent plant material of varied content

Juicy dandelion blossoms are one of this tortoise's favorite foods.

A feed rack can be useful, if space permits.

(field greens, romaine lettuce, high-fiber vegetable leaves, chopped vegetables such as carrots or kohlrabi).

Ten percent fat-free ground beef and five percent cooked corn meal or brown rice.

■ Food for carnivorous turtles:

Seventy-five percent animal protein, of the following composition: thirty percent freshwater fish, thirty percent heart, twenty percent cuttlefish, twenty percent liver.

The remaining twenty-five percent of the total is a combination of equal parts of greens, carrots, apples, brown rice, or cooked corn-meal.

Note: Chicken eggs or shrimp (both with shells) can be used to change the flavor or composition of the food. See what your turtle likes best.

Preparation is simple:

■ Rinse all ingredients well under running water.

■ For tortoises, puree the ingredients, adding a little

75

water, to a form thin mash with the consistency of honey.

■ For aquatic turtles, add the meat ingredients listed above.

■ Heat the mash to 175°F (80°C) (check the temperature with a food thermometer).

■ For each generous quart (one liter) of mash, add one level teaspoon of mineral/vitamin supplement (see table, page 73).

■ Stir the mash constantly while it cools to 140°F (60°C).

■ Now add a high-quality gelatin powder (from the grocery store), following package directions for aspic.

■ After it sets, cut the aspic into daily portions, place in plastic bags, and freeze.

Feeding Guidelines for Turtles

	How often?	How much?	What else?
Land Turtles (Tortoises), Young	Daily, morning, and afternoon.	The turtle should have about 10 minutes to eat each portion.	Healthy bone growth requires regular feeding of calcium, mineral/vitamin mixtures, and vitamin-rich food (see page 72).
Land Turtles Juvenile/Adult	Daily, morning, and afternoon.	The turtle should have about 20 minutes total to eat the two portions.	An egg-laying female needs extra calcium to build the egg shells. Give calcium supplements in the form of crushed eggshells ($\frac{1}{5}$ of a normal hen's egg, daily) for four weeks before and four weeks after she lays her eggs.
Water Turtles, Young	Daily, one or two times.	Daily ration: half the maximum amount that the turtle can eat at one time (see page 74).	Healthy bone growth requires regular feeding of calcium, mineral salt mixtures, and vitamin-rich food.
Water Turtles, Juvenile/Adult	Every other day; for adults, alternating two- and three-day intervals.	Half the amount that the turtle can eat in one meal before it is completely full.	An egg-laying female needs extra calcium to build the egg shells. Give calcium supplements in the form of crushed eggshells ($\frac{1}{5}$ of a normal hen's egg, daily) for four weeks before and four weeks after she lays her eggs.

Preventive Care and Health Problems

A pet turtle can live to a ripe old age. Unfortunately, studies have shown that more than half of all purchased turtles do not survive their first year in captivity. The primary reasons for this are insufficient knowledge about what turtles need and negligence of hygiene in the terrarium or aquarium.

Preventive Care

The three main causes of fatal illnesses in all turtles are:

■ drafts and of temperatures that are too cool;
■ calcium and vitamin deficiencies;
■ inadequate ultraviolet light.

Drafts: Never put a turtle on the floor of your home or in a terrarium or aquarium next to a window without a protected sunning spot. These areas are always subject to drafts.

Calcium and vitamin supplements: These are absolutely essential for the turtle's healthy development (see page 72).

Ultraviolet light: The ultraviolet light substitutes for sunlight and protects the turtle against bone diseases (see "Outdoor Enclosures for Tortoises," page 58).

PREVENTIVE CARE FOR TORTOISES

A clean terrarium is one of the most important prerequisites for your turtle's health. Water basins and the damp sand around them are perfect holding grounds for stomach and intestinal parasites, their eggs and larvae, and amoebas and bacteria of all kinds.

In the wild, turtles roam over wide areas and never again encounter the parasites that they excrete. In the terrarium, this is necessarily otherwise. Unless scrupulous cleanliness is maintained, the turtle will rein-

Young turtles generally have much brighter coloration than adult turtles.

A dark shell, like that of this painted turtle, absorbs the sun's warmth even on a cloudy day.

est its pathogens as it eats and drinks. For this reason, it is best to scrub the water basin and change the water every day and keep the area around it dry (by covering the sand with flat stones).

Change the sand around the bathing pool often (every four to eight weeks, as needed).

If your turtle eats sand or gravel in large quantities, it is probably suffering a mineral deficiency. Sand and gravel can cause fatal obstructions in the gastrointestinal tract. For this reason, be sure to provide vitamins, calcium, and trace elements on a regular basis (see page 72).

79

PREVENTIVE CARE FOR SEMIAQUATIC TURTLES

Hygiene is the first commandment in a terrarium for semiaquatic turtles. The water must be kept clean and the sand must not be wet. Remember that a turtle that lives in a river in the wild always has fresh water available. Even in a lake, turtle excrement or decomposing food scraps are relatively insignificant.

PREVENTIVE CARE FOR AQUATIC TURTLES

In an aquarium, clean water is the most important requirement; feces and food remnants can drastically reduce the water quality and make the turtle sick.

Sunbathing, a turtle extends all four legs to expose as much skin as possible.

TIP

▼

Clean water is important for a healthy turtle. Dirt, feces, and food remnants can be removed from the water with a tea strainer or a paper coffee filter. Muck in the aquarium water should be siphoned off with a piece of filter tubing.

These are preventive measures you can take:

1 Keep a small number of turtles in as much water as possible.

2 Thoroughly remove all food scraps and feces. Change water as necessary.

3 Install a filter with good filtering capacity (see page 56).

4 Avoid drafts that can penetrate through the openings of the terrarium. Turtles in warm water that must breathe colder air can easily catch cold or develop pneumonia (see respiratory distress, at right).

5 Strengthen your turtle's resistance by providing the proper water temperatures (75–79°F, 24–26°C) and a heat lamp above the land area.

Signs of Illness

Changes in behavior, such as apathy, and external symptoms, such as swollen eyelids, indicate that your turtle is sick.

The most common symptoms and diseases seen in turtles are described below.

RESPIRATORY DISTRESS

Symptoms: With extended neck and gaping mouth, the turtle makes cheeping, moaning, or snoring sounds; in between, it lowers its head in fatigue. Water turtles spend most of the time under the heat lamp, breathing with the mouth open.

Possible causes: Lung infection; constipation; difficulty laying eggs; gas in the stomach or intestines; bladder stones or uric acid calculus, preventing evacuation of the anal bladder; edema caused by kidney or heart disease.

Treatment: Do not add additional warmth! This would raise its metabolism, which can be acutely life threatening! You should take your turtle to the veterinarian at once for diagnosis and treatment.

Note: Fungal, bacterial, or herpes infections can cause the mouth to be coated with a mucous layer that inhibits breathing. Herpes in turtles is usually fatal. Only immediate quarantine, sanitary measures, and disinfection can save the other turtles.

DIARRHEA

Symptoms: Loose stools (see photo, page 83).

Possible causes: Improper diet, protozoal or fungal infection, worms.

Treatment: If there is no blood in the feces and the turtle is otherwise lively, first adjust its diet. Give no fruit; reduce the amount of greens and increase the proportion of dry food, such as leaves and hay. Instead of drinking water, offer chamomile tea or black tea (steeped for 10 minutes). If there is no improvement within two or three days, you must take the turtle to the veterinarian. Don't forget to bring a fresh stool sample (see page 105).

CHANGES IN URINE FOR TORTOISES

Symptoms: In most tortoises, the urine is a clear, aqueous substance containing white, mucous flecks of crystallized uric acid. Abnormal urine is viscous, and in advanced stages of illness the trace of white mucus is not seen. Later, small stones can be found in the urine. The tortoise is less lively than usual, and its joints, including the hind legs, are swollen (see drawing at right).

Cause: If a turtle does not drink enough water, its urine will become more concentrated, and greater amounts of uric acid will precipitate, forming crystals of increasing size. To conserve water, the tortoise's urine becomes thicker and thicker. In spite of the protective mucus in the urine, eventually the cell lining of the renal tubules and anal bladder is irritated by the crystal needles and becomes inflamed. Bacteria and protozoa can proliferate. Protein floccules, dead cells, and crystals form particles of increasing size, which block more and more renal corpuscles. The kidneys can no longer eliminate urea, which is toxic to cells, and uric acid, which causes gout. Toxic substances accumulate in the tortoise's body. Bladder stones or gout may develop, often accompanied by painful swelling of the joints.

Treatment: Take the tortoise to the veterinarian immediately; if left

Swollen joints indicate a kidney disease.

Excessive shedding, the result of too much vitamin A.

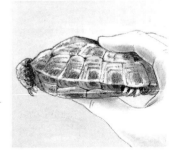

Soft shell, caused by too much vitamin D$_3$.

TIP

Do not hesitate to take your turtle to the veterinarian as soon as you notice something wrong. The earlier the veterinarian can make an exact diagnosis, the better the turtle's chances for recovery. Stool samples (see page 105) will aid in the diagnosis.

untreated, these illnesses are very painful and ultimately fatal. They can be prevented if the tortoise bathes several times a week; this allows it to take in plenty of water, which flushes the kidneys.

SHELL INJURIES

Cause: Usually accidents.

Treatment: Superficial abrasions of the horny layer are harmless. However, if the wound is so deep that it reaches the bone, the turtle must be taken to the veterinarian, who will remove the infected tissue and treat the bone wound daily. During this treatment, water turtles must be kept on dry newspaper and allowed into the water to eat and drink only for one hour each day. Very small turtles may be put in the water more often for short periods to prevent dehydration.

SWOLLEN EYES

Cause: Foreign bodies in the eye, injuries, vitamin A deficiency.

Vitamin A deficiency occurs almost only in aquatic turtles. It causes an increased exfoliation of cells of the harderian glands above the eyes. The eyelids become filled with an opaque white mass of conglutinated cells. The turtle cannot see, and it stops eating. Its eyelids bulge like a frog's, and it repeatedly rubs at its eyes with its front legs.

Treatment: Only by a veterinarian, who will rinse the turtle's eyes clean with a small syringe and inject vitamin A. For prevention, be sure your turtle eats a varied diet (see pages 70–77).

Note: All vitamin preparations containing vitamin A and vitamin D_3 must be administered in proportion

Well-formed feces of a healthy tortoise.

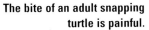

The bite of an adult snapping turtle is painful.

to the turtle's weight. If the dose is incorrect, these can be extremely toxic.

VITAMIN A POISONING

Symptom: Shedding, until the skin is raw (see drawing, page 82).

Treatment: Only by a veterinarian. The turtle must be kept very clean (risk of infection) and fed well. Screen to protect against flies in the terrarium or aquarium. Gen- tly coat the wounds with healing ointment. Avoid vitamin A preparations for several months.

VITAMIN D₃ POISONING

Symptoms: The turtle's shell becomes soft, with bleeding at the seams between scutes (see drawing, page 82).

Treatment: Veterinary attention is needed. Handle the turtle very gently. Pro-

Threads of mucus in the throat may be formed during eating, but they can also be a sign of illness.

Portrait of a radiated tortoise. Clear, bright eyes are a sign that the turtle is healthy.

vide regular mineral supplements. Do not allow access to sand and gravel. Grind boiled eggshells and sprinkle them over the turtle's food. Avoid vitamin D₃ preparations and provide regular ultraviolet light.

DIFFICULTY LAYING EGGS

Symptoms: Unsuccessful digging and unproductive straining while laying eggs.

Possible causes: Both mineral deficiencies and hormone deficiencies can cause this problem. Other possible causes include no proper egg deposition site, an egg that is malformed or too large, a kinked or twisted oviduct, obstruction by sand, injury to the cloaca, or a bladder stone.

Treatment: Only a veterinarian can determine what is causing the turtle to have difficulty laying eggs. Get immediate assistance!

Breeding Turtles

If given care appropriate to the species, turtles will reproduce even in captivity. However, you must remember not only to provide the female with vitamin and mineral supplements to permit her to form strong eggs, but to have an area and enough food for the young when they hatch. Once the young begin feeding, you can find new homes for the ones you do not wish to keep.

Sexual Maturity

European tortoises are sexually mature when they are three to five years old. European pond and river turtles are not sexually mature until they are 10 to 12 years old. Many other species reach reproductive age between these two extremes. Favorable living conditions can promote earlier sexual maturity.

The mating season for most species is between the end of April and the end of May. The mating instinct is triggered by factors such as increasing daylight, changing barometric pressure, and the sun's position.

Breeding Tips

■ For species that hibernate, be sure hibernation occurs (see pages 30–47).

■ If possible, keep a breeding pair in an outdoor enclosure during the summer months.

In the terrarium, you must make certain specific adjustments if you want your turtles to have offspring.

■ Turtles that do not hibernate should be separated for one to two months before you plan to breed them (keep them where they cannot see, hear, or smell each other).

■ Three months before you want them to mate, decrease the artificial daylight provided by the overhead spot lamp and other terrarium lighting to just eight hours a day. After two months, increase the lighting gradually over three to four weeks, to 10 to 12 hours daily.

■ At first, reduce the air and/or water temperature by about 8–10°F (4–5°C). Turn off additional heat sources, such as spot lamps and underground heating mats.

A turtle can identify a suitable
mate by its odor, which differs
from species to species.

■ As you extend the hours of daylight, gradually increase the air and/or water temperature over three to four weeks. In the final week, turn on the overhead spot lamp and/or the heating mat.

■ In the final week, give your turtles a spring rain. Twice a day, spray the terrarium and the turtles with a plant mister (see "Tip," page 89). This increases the humidity. Higher humidity, along with the rising temperature, helps to trigger the mating urge.

■ When you give your turtles fresh, tender food while increasing the temperature, they will begin their courtship behavior.

Fertilization

The male has already formed its sperm during the previous summer and stored them during hibernation.

The female likewise establishes her eggs in summer and completes their development in springtime, after the winter rest. Before the shell is formed, the eggs are fertilized. This does not require mating each time; many females can store sperm for up to four years. Thus, it could happen that a turtle you acquire and keep by itself would lay fertilized eggs after one to three years.

Top: This Hermann's tortoise has cracked open its egg using its *egg tooth*, or *caruncle*, on the tip of its beak.

Bottom: It can take several hours for the shell to open completely.

Free! Still somewhat scrunched up from the confined space of the egg, the tortoise goes out into the world.

Artificial Incubation

All turtles lay their eggs on land, even those that are otherwise entirely aquatic, such as the soft-shelled turtle (see page 43).

Aquatic turtles must be able to leave the water, for example, by crawling up a ramp, to deposit and bury their eggs in the sand. Fill a box with sand and place it next to the water. The box should be rectangular and at least twice as long as the turtle. The sand should be at least as deep as the turtle's shell is long.

Terrestrial turtles bury their eggs in the terrarium if the sand is as deep as their shell length. It's a good idea to have an area like this, with warm, slightly moist sand, in every terrarium.

Many species deposit all the eggs at once, others at intervals of five to ten days. After the eggs are laid, you should remove them to safety so the turtle won't damage them in the confined space of the terrarium or egg-laying box. Mark the top of each egg with a soft lead pencil. They must not be turned for the rest of the incubation period; otherwise, the yolk will crush the embryo, and it will die. It is also helpful to number the eggs, if they are laid at relatively long intervals. This will make it possible to calculate when you can expect the hatchlings to emerge.

The incubation chamber consists of a clear plastic container, half filled with slightly moist vermiculite (from the hardware store) or simple builders sand. Bury the eggs halfway in the vermiculite or sand. Then close the lid of the container. The humidity inside will rise to the 100-percent level that is needed. Lift the lid once a day and fan a little fresh air into the container. To keep condensation on the under-

side of the lid from dripping onto the eggs (which can kill the embryos), tilt the container, setting one edge on a matchbox or similar object so the condensation can run off the lid at an angle.

Place the container of eggs in a room where the ambient temperature is 82°F (28°C). This may be your furnace room, the heated shelter in your outdoor turtle enclosure, or a heated quarantine terrarium.

Note: The following arrangement offers ideal temperatures for incubating turtle eggs: Place two bricks in a plastic terrarium. Add water to just below the top of the bricks. Set the plastic container of eggs on the bricks. Heat the water to 82°F (28°C) with an aquarium heater. Cover the aquarium with a pane of glass. A small wedge made of wood will allow the condensation to run off. When you need to add water, add only

The bog turtle *Clemmys muhlenbergii* grows to only five inches (11 cm) long. Like most pond and river turtles, it prefers to copulate in the water.

Mating
How do turtles mate?

In the wild, turtles are usually solitary creatures. Only during the mating period, from April to May, do males and females get together to reproduce. Because turtles have a keen sense of smell, they recognize a possible mate by its odor. When a male has found a female, he slowly circles around her. If the female turtle won't stop moving to let the male approach, he will bite her front legs. He does this to get her to stop and lie down. If the female doesn't cooperate, the male will ram his shell against hers. Now the female may lie down, indicating that she is ready to mate. Finally, the male mounts her from the rear and deposits his sperm inside her. He may make hissing or whistling noises while he does this. The photograph on pages 86 and 87 shows two tortoises mating.

A male tortoise who is kept alone shows the same behavior. During the mating period, he may even view your shoe or a rock as a possible mate.

warm water to avoid breaking the glass of the heater.

The baby turtles hatch after 30 days (for soft-shelled turtles), 90 days (for painted turtles), or even 150 days (for snake-necked turtles). Some tortoise eggs may take even longer.

Caring for Baby Turtles

It can take turtles one to three days to hatch. During this time, the eggs must not be disturbed. Leave the hatchlings in the incubator until the yolk sac on the navel has shriveled and fallen off (it may take a few days). Of course, this requires an incubator of adequate size.

The hatchlings are raised separately from their parents. They need the same living conditions as the adult turtles (see pages 30–47). However, it will be about a week before the baby turtles eat. It takes that long for their metabolisms to adjust from digesting the yolk to digesting solid food. Mince their food somewhat smaller so the young turtles can grasp it easily. Provide the necessary calcium and vitamins (see dietary supplements, page 72).

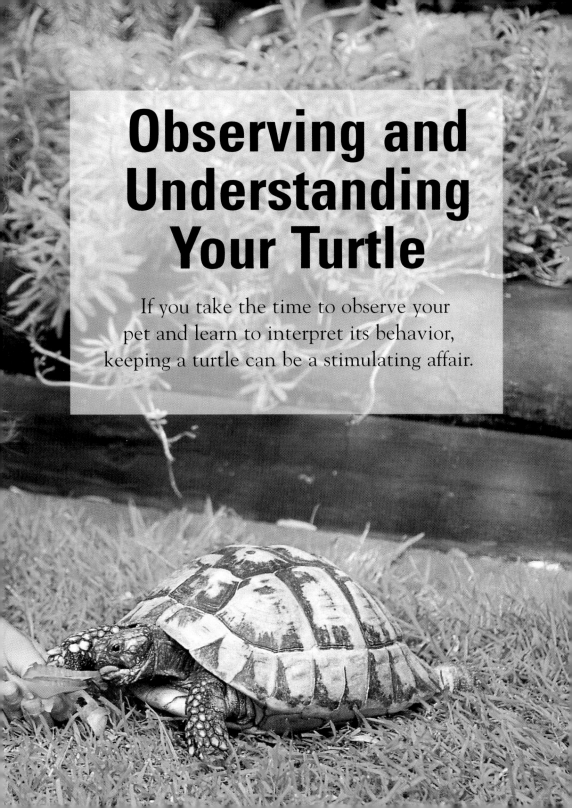

Observing and Understanding Your Turtle

If you take the time to observe your pet and learn to interpret its behavior, keeping a turtle can be a stimulating affair.

What Turtles Can Do

What a mistake to assume that turtles are boring! It's true that they can't make themselves understood, as dogs and cats can, by using their voices. But their body language can be very expressive of their moods and feelings at any given time.

Body Language

Turtles in captivity often exhibit the following behaviors:

Pacing back and forth or climbing up the terrarium walls: A turtle may cruise endlessly along the wall of its enclosure, as if looking for a way out. Or it may go to a corner and try to climb out over the edge. Similarly, an aquatic turtle may swim back and forth along the glass sides of the aquarium. This can be a clear signal that the turtle is not happy in its surroundings. Perhaps the climate in the terrarium or aquarium is not right (see pages 30–47). Other causes of this behavior may include too small an enclosure; hunger; boredom with its environment, possibly because there are no features to climb on, or loud noises in the room (see page 58). If a newly acquired turtle has just moved into its terrarium or aquarium, it may simply be curiously investigating its territory. After a day or two, however, the turtle should have calmed down (see page 110).

Digging in the ground: If your tortoise keeps scraping at the ground with its hind legs and if its size is between half-grown and adult, you may have a female who is trying to lay eggs. This behavior can even be observed when there is no earth to dig in. For example, if you place the tortoise on a smooth surface, it will still scrape and scratch. If

TIP

If your female aquatic turtle suddenly begins to swim restlessly back and forth along the aquarium glass, it may be ready to lay eggs. You should immediately provide a suitable place to do this (see page 89).

Something smells good! Turtles use their keen sense of smell to orient themselves.

Portrait of a big-headed turtle. The hook on its upper jaw helps it to climb around under water.

this happens, you should immediately provide a suitable place for the tortoise to deposit her eggs (see page 88).

Rooting around in the gravel at the bottom of the aquarium: Aquatic turtles do this when foraging for food. You can take this as a sign that your turtle is still hungry or is already hungry again.

Stretching out flat on all fours: The turtle extends its extremities, including its head and tail, as far as it can out of its shell. The head usually rests flat on the ground, eyes closed. This behavior can be seen especially outdoors in the sunshine and under the overhead spot lamp in the terrarium or aquarium. Your turtle is sunbathing.

Caution: If your turtle spends all day in this position under the heat lamp or

95

ultraviolet lamp, you should be concerned.

Pick up the turtle to see if it actively assumes a defensive posture (see table, page 29). If it does not but, instead, seems to be listless, it is probably sick and must be taken to the veterinarian.

Standing tall, legs extended, head held high: Your turtle is curious and is taking this posture to get a better look around. This position also makes it easier to defecate.

Pulling in the head and legs: If the turtle suddenly pulls in its head and legs, it has been alarmed.

Climbing up against objects: The turtle raises its forelegs to mount round objects such as large stones, the toe of your shoe, or the like. Your turtle may be a male with an urge to mate; in the absence of a suitable partner, he is treating these objects as substitutes. An unreceptive female will flee such advances in haste. If you keep several turtles, the terrarium must be structured in such a way that the individual turtles have opportunities to retreat. If necessary, the male can be temporarily housed in a separate terrarium.

One turtle rams another with its shell: The aggressor may approach diagonally from the front, perhaps nipping at the other turtle's legs or neck. A male turtle

Top: Flipped in midclimb, the turtle has landed on its back.

Bottom: The turtle pushes with its head to begin to right itself.

Top: The branch provides support for the maneuver.

Bottom: Done! In exactly 38.6 seconds, the turtle is right side up again.

often does this as a prelude to mating. The male is signaling the female to hold still, lie down, and accept his advances. If the aggression leads to injuries, you should separate the turtles.

An aquatic turtle approaches another from the front, hovering with the front legs extended and quivering. Occasionally, this behavior is preceded by intensive sniffing of the tail area. This is also courtship behavior; the male is attempting to impress the female. If the female is not receptive, the male may nip at her skin. If there is a danger of injury, the male should be temporarily separated from the female.

A land-dwelling turtle burrows into hiding: If it also stops eating, the turtle may be showing signs of preparing to hibernate. This happens in autumn, when the days are much shorter and the sun is low in the sky. Horsfield's tortoises also exhibit this behavior before estivation, a period of limited activity in the heat of the summer (see page 65). At other times of year, such behavior can also indicate that the turtle is ill. In that case, take the turtle to the veterinarian at once.

The Senses

The sense of smell is

97

highly developed, leading a turtle unerringly to a suitable mate and to its feeding spot. The smell of a particular food is a critical factor in determining whether a turtle will like it.

Aquatic turtles can smell just as well under water as on land, and they also use their sense of smell to navigate. By moving the floor of the mouth, they pump water through the nose into the mouth and let it flow out of the mouth.

Vision is very keen, enabling turtles to detect food and enemies from afar. For example, a Hermann's tortoise can spy a yellow dandelion, one of its favorite foods, from a great distance. When nearby, however, it tends to rely more on its good sense of smell.

Many turtles can also recognize a familiar person from far away and will come closer.

Hearing is less acute. Turtles hear low-pitched sounds best. You may be able to entice your turtle to approach by calling it in a deep voice or by playing low notes on a musical instrument. I have seen a

turtle that learned to come for a treat when its owner played the piano.

A turtle also senses vibrations (footsteps, falling rocks) in the ground; the vibrations are conducted through the legs and shell to the inner ear.

Turtles do not have an external ear; the eardrum lies directly below the skin. For this reason, it is often difficult to identify the ear. The ear is located slightly behind the jaws and is often covered by leathery skin or by scales (see photo, page 68).

Is winter over yet? A Hermann's tortoise cautiously emerges from its winter quarters.

98

Once out, it will rest for a few more days before resuming full activity.

The Turtle's Shell

A turtle's most striking feature is its shell. However, you must not make the mistake of thinking that a turtle is literally armor-plated. For the most part, the shell consists of living material that can be injured.

Bony plates constitute the supporting structure of the shell, and are made up of areas of ossified skin, fused together with parts of the vertebrae, ribs, and shoulder girdle. The shell is thus an integral part of the turtle's skeleton. This vaulted bone structure is covered by a membrane of connective tissue.

This layer is very sensitive—anyone who has been kicked in the shin, directly on the similar layer surrounding the shinbone, knows how sensitive—and is protected only by the horny shield plates.

These horny plates, the *scutes,* are the only parts of the shell made of dead tissue, comparable to that of a human's fingernails.

Note: The individual scutes are joined by growth areas, usually lighter in color. Here, the horny layer is much thinner and offers little protection. These regions are highly sensitive, and they should not be scratched, probed with a fingernail, or scrubbed with a brush.

The shell of a tortoise grows more bumpy with age, and the scutes become thicker. However, the scutes wear down uniformly as the tortoise rubs against roots, thorns, and stones in its wanderings or as it burrows into the ground. As long as a tortoise is healthy, it will not lose entire scutes.

In many aquatic species, however, such as *Chrysemis, Cuora,* and *Chelodina*

(see pages 30–47), it is normal for thin, horny layers to be sloughed from the scutes.

The soft-shelled turtles have a distinctively reduced shell (see page 44). The flat, bony carapace is covered only by a tough, leathery skin, with no scutes. The plastron consists of somewhat broader bones in the region of the hip and shoulder girdles. Most of the underbelly is thus covered only by soft skin.

An amazing feature is that a soft-shelled turtle, buried in sand, can breathe through its skin, taking in oxygen and releasing carbon dioxide into the water. As a result, soft-shells are also very sensitive to dirty water in the aquarium or to shell injuries, which can quickly become infected.

Hinged joints are another distinctive feature of turtle shells, as seen in the box turtles (page 35). This modification carries the shell's

Painted turtles love to bask in the sunshine. They can be kept outdoors from the end of May to September.

Swimming
Can tortoises swim?

No, unfortunately not. Many tortoises drown in deep water because the weight of their shell holds them down.

If a land-dwelling turtle ever accidentally tumbles into your garden pond, you must act quickly. Take the tortoise out of the water at once, and hold it with its head pointing down. This will help the tortoise to empty the water from its lungs. Then take it to a veterinarian right away.

The water in your tortoise's wading pool should only be deep enough to come halfway up its shell. This will allow it to breathe at all times. For young tortoises, you should provide a stepping stone that will help them climb in and out of the pool. The drawing on page 53 shows how to do this.

Giant tortoises live in areas with very limited food supplies and are resourceful at finding food. These tortoises feed partially on marine algae. The algae grow in the sea, but at low tide the turtles can easily graze among them. When high tide comes, raising the water level again, the turtles simply let themselves be carried back onto the shore.

protective function to amazing perfection. Normally—for example, in the case of Hermann's tortoise—the turtle pulls its head, arms, and legs into its shell, leaving the tough skin of its legs exposed. The box turtle, however, can raise the front and rear sections of its plastron like a drawbridge, closing the shell up tight and offering complete protection all around.

Similar mechanisms are seen in other turtles mentioned in this book, such as the common mud turtle (page 54) and the hinge-backed tortoises with their jointed carapace (pages 34 and 36).

Note: Be wary of purchasing young to half-grown turtles, supposedly of a very rare species, that have quite bumpy shells, with individual bones or scutes forming rounded cones. These are probably deformed turtles suffering from malnutrition; they may also have metabolic disorders. Do not buy a turtle like this under any circumstances.

In fairness, it should be noted that certain species

of tortoises have quite pronounced horny pyramids on the individual scutes in advanced age. Furthermore, some species of freshwater turtles from America and Asia, such as the diamond-backed terrapin (*Malaclemys*) and juvenile roofed turtles or Mississippi map turtles, naturally have keeled carapaces (see page 41). Often, the common names of these turtles refer to this distinctive feature.

The color of the shell may vary, depending on a number of different factors.

For example, young painted turtles are grass green, though the adults have a dark brown shell. Turtles of many other species also change shell color as they get older, although not quite as dramatically as the painted turtles.

Captive turtles are almost always lighter in color than those in their native habitat. The more brilliant and intense coloration of turtles in the wild can be attributed to the influence of natural sunlight, a more varied diet,

and the sheen acquired as the turtle's shell rubs against rocks, thorns, and roots in its terrain.

The Beak and Claws

Beak: Instead of teeth, turtles have jaws with sharp horny edges that they use to grind and shred plant and animal matter. The first time a turtle uses its beak is when it hatches from its egg (see photo on page 88). These horny jaws are continually worn down and grow back.

Because the jaws are very powerful, large turtles in

The box turtle has a hinge at the front of its plastron and another at the back, allowing it to draw its shell up tight.

When danger threatens and when it sleeps, the box turtle closes itself completely into its shell.

particular can bite a person hard enough to draw blood (or even remove a finger). Sometimes the horny edges of the jaw are curved to form a hooked bite.

In certain species, such as *Pyxidea mouhoti* (see page 46), only the tip of the upper jaw is elongated; it serves as a climbing aid.

In many land-dwelling species, the horny jaws have serrated edges. These enable the beasts to easily cut and crush plant parts with tougher fibers.

Claws: Like the horny jaws, these continue to grow and wear. Be sure to provide a hard substrate in the terrarium and outdoor enclosure so the claws will wear down properly (see pages 50–63).

If the claws are too long, they may become snagged in cracks and possibly even be torn from their beds. This could result in serious inflammation that will need veterinary attention.

In some aquatic turtles, it is possible to differentiate between the sexes by the length of their front claws. Males have long front claws while females have short claws.

Getting Your Turtle Properly Settled

A newly acquired turtle should be quarantined (see page 58) before you place it in its terrarium or aquarium, even if it seems to be fit as a fiddle. You will not be able to tell whether your turtle has a worm infestation or an infection just by looking at it. A turtle that excretes parasite eggs into its terrarium or aquarium will continue to reinfest itself, and infectious diseases can be spread to other turtles of the same species.

First, a Bath!

Before putting the turtle in quarantine, you should give it a good bath. At the same time, inspect your turtle thoroughly once more for injuries and parasites. Ticks or mites can lodge especially in the folds of the skin (see drawing, page 66).

Terrestrial and semiterrestrial turtles should be placed in a good-sized bowl of warm water (79°F, 26°C). Be sure the turtle can hold its head above water; you can allow it to drink. The warm water will slowly loosen any remaining bits of dirt from its body. A bath of 10 to 20 minutes is generally adequate.

An aquatic turtle should also have a bath before being placed in its quarantine aquarium. This will keep the water in the quarantine quarters clean longer.

After the bath, put the turtle in its quarantine terrarium or aquarium and let it creep into its hiding place for a while. (A tortoise should be dried first, because evaporation of the water

"The way to the heart is through the stomach." Fresh greens entice even a timid turtle out of hiding.

On very hot summer days, some tortoises kept outdoors will happily dig themselves into the dirt.

could cause it to lose body heat, stressing it further.) Allow the turtle to stay in hiding until it emerges of its own accord. You can speed the process by offering fresh food every day.

Stool Samples

A turtle's feces provides information about whether it has worms. Have a stool sample analyzed by a veterinarian or a veterinary laboratory facility. Infectious diseases or other ailments can be detected only by carefully observing your pet (see page 78).

The turtle must remain in quarantine until it can be officially declared healthy.

How to take a stool sample: A veterinarian can give you special containers for stool specimens. Take a stool sample every day for three days. Add a drop of water to each container so the sample will not dry out and lose its value for testing. The oldest sample must be no more than five days old when it is submitted for analysis. Until then, keep the stool samples in the refrigerator to prevent the growth of mold, which would also make them unfit for diagnostic use.

Note: Turtles normally excrete a whitish yellow urine, possibly tinged with pink, of a viscous to crumbly consistency. The urine is occasionally emitted separately from the feces, but may also be excreted at the same time. Urine samples are not useful for determining whether your turtle has parasites.

Housing Turtles Together

Because turtles by nature are solitary creatures, it is especially important to provide adequate space for each turtle in the terrarium or aquarium, as well as enough hiding places and basking spots for all. This is the only way to prevent scuffles. It's a good idea to provide one or two more sunning islands and hideaways than there are turtles living in the terrarium or aquarium.

TIP

▼

To transport a turtle safely, for example, when taking it to the veterinarian, place it in a sack made of cotton or linen. Set the sack with the turtle inside—right side up—in a cardboard box. In winter, a hot-water bottle under the bag will keep the turtle from catching cold.

Turn the sack inside out, so the turtle won't get tangled in the loose threads along the seams.

A long-established inhabitant that has a new turtle introduced to its living quarters may vigorously defend its territory—that is, the entire terrarium or aquarium—against the newcomer, possibly intimidating it to the point that the newcomer stays in hiding and even refuses to eat. In that case, the old-timer should be sent to quarantine quarters (see page 58) for about two weeks. During that time, the newly acquired turtle can explore the territory, gain confidence, and become less readily intimidated. If the turtles continue to do battle despite all your precautions, you will have no choice but to separate them permanently.

Note: One way to help turtles get along is to keep them in an outdoor enclosure in the summer months. In this larger, more natural environment, it's much easier for the turtles to avoid each other and hide from one another.

You will find that some turtles tolerate sharing a terrarium or aquarium with another of the same species only during the mating season.

Be aware that a male will pursue a female with particular intensity during this time. Even in a spacious terrarium or an outdoor enclosure, it will be impossible for the female to elude the male forever because he will keep tracking her down by her scent. You should remove the male temporarily.

In winter, tuck a hot-water bottle under the cloth sack to keep the turtle from catching cold.

Interacting with Your Pet

If you're looking for lots of playing and cuddling, a turtle is not the right pet. On the other hand, a turtle owner can spend many fascinating hours observing the creature's behavior. For this, of course, it's essential to give your turtle plenty of diversity in its living quarters. You may also be able to establish quite personal contact with these primitive reptiles. They will become tame to your hand if you interact with them regularly, and they may even learn to come when called to get their food.

Hide and Seek

In the wild, land-dwelling turtles roam widely in their search for food. In the terrarium, space is limited, and the tortoise does not need to forage because you feed it. Nevertheless, even in a terrarium it is possible to keep your turtle on the go and challenge its keen sense of smell.

Hide a treat or two—dandelion or daisy blossoms, lettuce leaves, a bit of banana, a slice of tomato, or a sprig of parsley—some-where in the terrarium, in addition to your pet's usual ration. You might tuck a tasty morsel under a rock, on a root, or in one of the hideaways you have constructed for your tortoise. The more varied the terrain and the hiding places in the terrarium, the more interesting the search will be for your pet. Lured by the smell of its favorite tidbits, your tortoise will eagerly take up the hunt. Given a good supply of treats, you can entertain your tortoise for hours in its terrarium with this game.

Note: While it's important to give your turtle adequate exercise, letting it roam freely indoors is not a good idea. There is too great a risk that it will be exposed to drafts, catch a cold, become stranded in the back of a closet or under a piece of furniture and die (see page 78).

Semiaquatic and aquatic turtles can also be stimulated to exercise with special treats.

One way to do this is to build a mealworm machine. Take a plexiglass tube about 8 inches (20 cm) long, and

Playtime. Of course, you should never leave cats and turtles together unattended.

drill a row of holes 5/64 inch (2 mm) in diameter along it. Hang the tube above the water with wires, holes down. Put several mealworms in the container, and plug each end with a cork. The mealworms will crawl along the tube until they discover the holes. Then they will work their way out, falling into the water at irregular intervals. The turtle below will pounce on this unexpected snack. Because it doesn't know just when the next yummy tidbit will appear, it will hover watchfully nearby, then nimbly go after the mealworm when it drops into the water.

Note: Mealworms are easy to raise at home, but you can also buy them at a pet store.

Taming a Turtle to Your Touch

Food is the most important element in the life of a turtle. This means that the best way to entice your turtle to come to you and be tamed is to provide a tasty snack.

Observe your pet to see what foods it likes best. Take the treat between your thumb and forefinger and hold it out to your tortoise; for aquatic turtles, hold it at the surface of the water.

The turtle will first sniff cautiously at the food, which also smells a little like your hand. Then it will take a few tentative nibbles. Try not to make any sudden movements now, or you will startle your pet and make it wary of you. Usually, however, most turtles soon become accustomed to your hand and your person. In the future, your turtle will associate your arrival with something good to eat.

Note: It's hard to say how long it will take before a turtle is tame to your touch. It depends in part on whether your turtle was already used to humans before it came to you and whether it had positive experiences. However, many turtles never lose their natural wariness; others become timid again over the summer if they are kept outdoors.

A turtle can't see very well close up. Your pet may accidentally chomp on your finger instead of the dandelion.

Coming When Called

Will my turtle learn to come when I call its name?

A turtle may learn to recognize your voice and know, from your inflection, that you are calling it. But a turtle cannot hear as well as a dog, for instance. Your turtle is best able to hear low tones. You should keep this in mind when you name your pet. Choose a name with lots of *O* and *U* sounds, but no high, clear sounds, like *I*. Sandra let her turtle choose its own name. She sat down on the grass a little way away from her pet. Then she slowly read from a list of names she had written down: Goliath, Tutu, Otto, Bobo, Cooper. What name do you think the turtle picked? As Sandra was reading the names a second time, the turtle came over to her. She had just said "Otto." Of course, the turtle didn't really know it was choosing its name. Instead, it had just noticed the dandelion Sandra had picked while she was reciting the names. Dandelions are Otto's favorite food.

Teaching Your Turtle Tricks

Once you have found that your turtle likes to eat from your hand, you can try to teach it more advanced tricks.

Climbing on your hand: Put a tidbit on your wrist (palm up). Hold your open hand out in front of your turtle like a ramp, and let it clamber up to reach the tempting treat.

Coming in response to music: Turtles are best able to hear low tones. You might be able to teach your turtle to come for food when you ring a bell, for example, or play deep notes on a musical instrument. This demonstration is an especially effective way to show off for visitors. However, don't be disappointed if your turtle doesn't learn this particular trick. Many turtles won't respond to bribery; that doesn't mean they're any less captivating as pets.

Problems and How to Solve Them

Turtles are generally tolerant pets. Most problems arise from improper care or a lack of information about what the turtle needs.

Pacing or Swimming Back and Forth

Situation: The turtle paces or swims back and forth for hours or days along the glass wall of the terrarium or aquarium.

Possible causes:
1. If you have just put the turtle into an unfamiliar enclosure, it is curiously exploring its new territory. This behavior should stop after one or two days.
2. Did you recently modify the equipment or the decorations, or have you just done a thorough cleaning? The new situation may be too warm, too dry, or too loud for your pet. Strong odors or vibrations are also unsettling (see page 94).
3. Do several turtles live in the terrarium or aquarium? As they grow, and especially when they reach puberty, one turtle may dominate the

other, putting it under pressure by its mere presence (or by aggressive courtship). The besieged turtle will become agitated and seek safety in flight, which, of course, is impossible in an enclosed space.
4. Is your pet a half-grown or adult female? Even with no male around, a female may develop unfertilized eggs. If she is unable to lay her eggs, she will be distressed (see page 85). This causes agitated behavior.

Remedies:
For **1**: Distract the turtle by providing a suitable hiding place and fresh food. It should calm down after a day or two.
For **2**: Review your turtle's climatic needs (see pages 30–47). Use an accurate thermometer to check conditions. Avoid vibrations by fastening equipment to the wall of the tank or placing it on a nearby table. Sometimes a thick foam pad under the terrarium or aquarium is all that is needed.
Check whether strong odors, such as disinfectants

or perfumes (essential oils), might be bothering your turtle.
For **3**: Try separating the turtles until the mating season is over. If the situation does not improve in late summer and fall, you may have to separate them permanently.
For **4**: It's essential to provide an egg-laying site immediately (see page 89).

Staying Hidden

Situation: The turtle spends days on end in hiding.

Possible causes:
1. Newly acquired turtles need time to get used to their new environment. This behavior is normal.
2. The turtle may be nocturnal, active at night and hiding during the day.
3. Your pet may be preparing to hibernate. The Horsfield's tortoise also behaves this way in summer (see page 65).
4. This behavior is also a typical sign that a turtle is ill. You should be concerned if your pet is weak and loses weight, wheezes

as it breathes, or occasionally deposits foul-smelling stools.

Remedies:

For **1**: Leave the turtle alone for a day or two, but keep offering it fresh food (see page 70).

For **2**: Find out whether your turtle is in fact nocturnal (see species profiles, pages 30–47). Accept your pet's natural rhythm. Don't disturb it during the day; feed it at night or early in the morning.

For **3**: Determine whether your turtle may need to hibernate (see pages 30–47). If it does, begin the necessary preparations right away (see page 65).

For **4**: If your turtle is ill, don't hesitate to take it to the veterinarian. If the feces smells foul, it's a good idea to take along a stool sample (see page 106).

Staying Too Long Under the Heat Lamp

Situation: Your turtle may spend longer than usual (one or two hours a day is normal) under the heat lamp.

Possible causes:
1. f the turtle is lively and has a good appetite, the climate outside the warm zone may be colder than recommended for the particular species (see pages 30–47).
2. If it also seems listless and refuses to eat, it is probably sick.

Remedies:
For **1**: Review the turtle's temperature requirements (see pages 30–47).

For **2**: A sick turtle attempts to activate its body's defense system by raising its body temperature. Especially with young turtles, there is a risk of dehydration. You should also be careful about using a new ultraviolet lamp. If the exposure time is too long or the light is too close, the turtle's skin and eyes may be damaged by sunburn. If in doubt, consult a veterinarian.

Swallowing Sand and Gravel

Cause: Turtles in the wild naturally ingest some sand with their food. This does not harm them at all. In captivity, however, aquatic turtles in particular often swallow gravel. If they ingest too much, a life-threatening intestinal blockage may develop.

Tussling turtles: Each tries to flip the other onto its back.

Remedies: Change the aquarium substrate immediately, using fine sand instead of gravel.

Feed the turtle often, choosing high-fiber foods, which will provide bulk around the stones in the intestine and facilitate elimination. At the same time, provide additional calcium and trace elements with the food (see page 72).

Biting Each Other

Situation: Two or more turtles sharing a terrarium or aquarium pester and nip at each other, causing injuries.

Causes:
1. If you own a sexually mature pair of the same or related species, this may be courtship behavior, especially if it occurs between April and July.
2. If you own turtles of different species, possibly both male, aggressive

Large and small turtles get along well, but they should be fed separately (see page 74).

behavior can have many different causes. In some cases, males will do battle out of rivalry. Occasionally, a male with a high sex drive may regard another male with a weaker sex drive as a potential mate and attempt to force it into submission. These advances may include biting. Because it is unable to flee, the victim may sustain fatal injuries.

Startled, a Horsfield's tortoise pulls its head inside its shell for protection.

Remedy: If the battles continue, you must separate incompatible couples as well as rivalrous males.

Shedding

Situation: The turtle loses large flakes of skin from all its soft body surfaces.

Causes: For a tortoise, this is a symptom of illness, possibly resulting from a vitamin deficiency caused by improper diet (see page 72). It may also be caused by ultraviolet light that is too strong.

For water turtles, on the other hand, shedding is a normal phenomenon, occurring regularly once or twice a year when thin, almost transparent pieces of skin may be seen sloughing off. Of course, a fresh, fully intact new skin surface must be visible as the dead skin flakes off.

Remedies: For a tortoise, discontinue exposure to ultraviolet light, and take your pet to the veterinarian for treatment. For water turtles, inspect the condition of new skin; if in doubt, consult a veterinarian.

Algae Growing on the Shell

Situation: Especially in aquatic turtles, the shell may develop a furry coating of bluish green or green filamentous algae.

115

Cause: This phenomenon is almost never seen in land turtles. In water turtles, however, it occurs especially when they are kept in an outdoor terrarium, garden pond, or indoor aquarium under strong sunlight.

Remedy: Algae growth on the shell is harmless, especially because aquatic turtles shed the upper covering of the shell scutes once or twice a year. However, the coating does mask the surface of the shell, making it difficult for you to inspect for possible damage and disease. As a result, you will need to be particularly observant of your turtle's behavior.

Dead Embryos

Experienced turtle handlers can tell even in the first few days whether a turtle egg is fertilized or not. After three or four weeks, however, this will be evident to novices as well.

Pick up the turtle egg (be careful to keep the marked end up; see page 89) and hold it between your thumb and forefinger in front of a strong light, such as a desk lamp.

In the early stages of development, fertilized eggs can be recognized by blood vessels inside them; later, the interior is relatively dark.

Unfertilized eggs show a very light area that is a pocket of air and a somewhat darker area of dried-up yolk.

Unfertilized eggs gradually weigh less as they dry out, while fertilized eggs keep getting heavier.

Cause: The death of an embryo in an egg is usually not related to the incubation conditions (see "Incubating the Eggs," page 88). More often, the mother did not get enough vitamins or other important nutrients; as a result, the developing embryo is also malnourished and weak and finally dies within the egg. This may happen even just before it is time to hatch.

If you should encounter this, please carefully review the care you give your turtles, and improve the

Only a few days old, this tortoise weighs just two-thirds of an ounce (20 grams).

What Turtles Like
How can you make your turtle happy?

The nicest thing you can do for your pet turtle is to be sure that its terrarium or aquarium is always kept clean. To entertain your pet, give it plenty of places to hide. Land turtles like to crawl under roots; water turtles enjoy sunning themselves on a safe island, such as a piece of driftwood. If startled, they can scoot quickly into the water. Make an obstacle course for your tortoise, using stones or thick branches. Food tidbits hidden in the terrarium will amuse your turtle for a long time. Water turtles will have fun with a resinous swamp log; you can buy this in a pet store. Be sure the food you give your turtle is fresh.

turtles, shedding the upper layer of the scutes once or twice a year is normal, as long as the horny layer below is intact.

Remedies: Take your tortoise to the veterinarian immediately. While it is being treated, keep it in a quarantine terrarium and disinfect its enclosure. For an aquatic turtle, this will be necessary only if the turtle is sick, for example, if the same conditions described above for tortoises are observed beneath the old scute as it falls off.

mother turtle's supply of vitamins, trace elements, and natural sunlight.

Scutes Detaching from Shell

Situation: A land turtle may have loose scutes on the shell, with a watery pink liquid beneath that shifts when the scute is pressed. In aquatic turtles, individual scutes or even the entire carapace may be sloughed off.

Causes: In land turtles, this is caused by disease, possibly a bacterial or fungal infection. In aquatic

My Turtle

Place a favorite photo here.

_____

Name

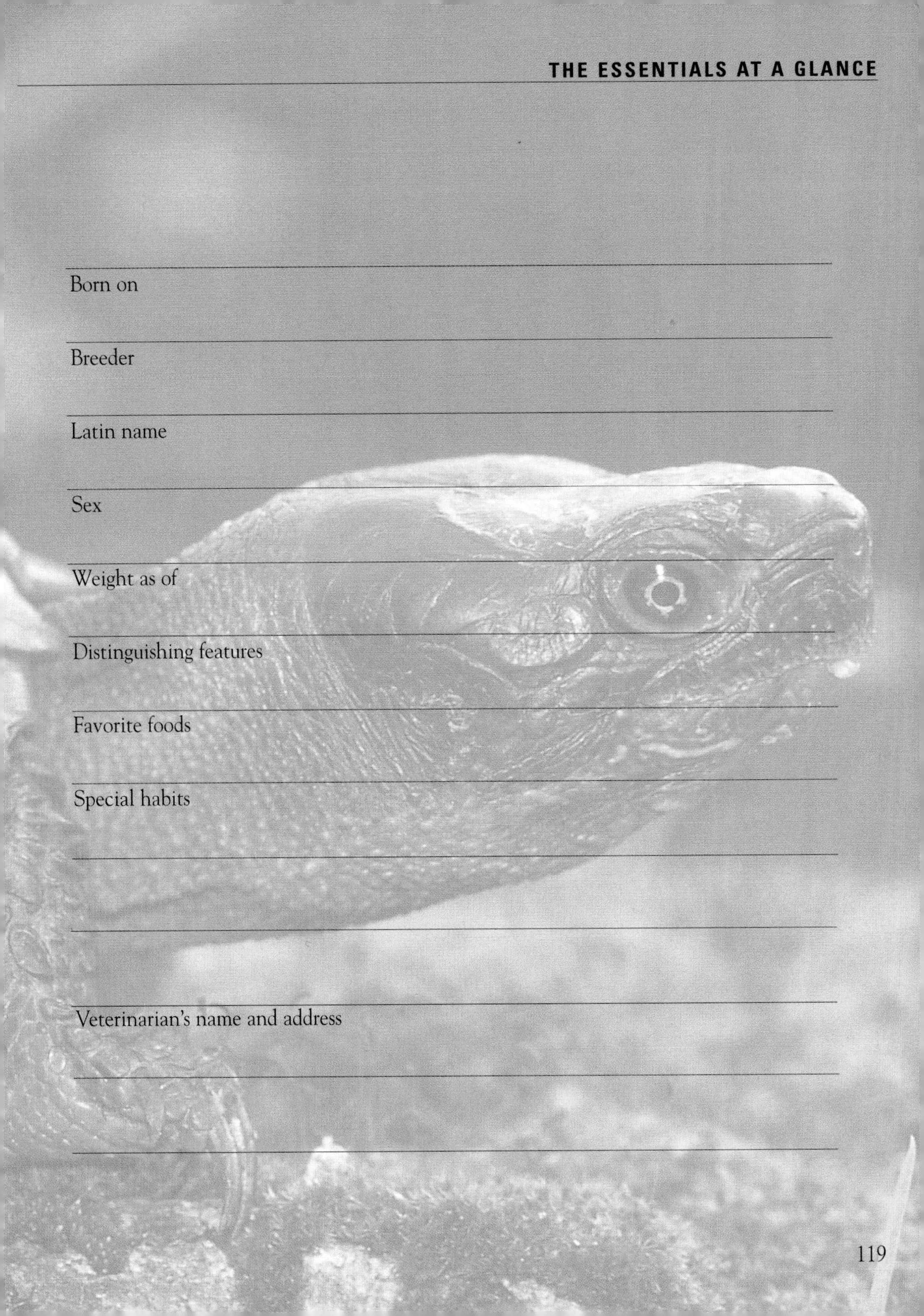

Born on

Breeder

Latin name

Sex

Weight as of

Distinguishing features

Favorite foods

Special habits

Veterinarian's name and address

**Juicy tomatoes quench
a tortoise's thirst.**

**A male Horsfield's tortoise
approaches the
object of his
affections.**

(top) This little fellow will right himself in no time.

(bottom) A tortoise coming out of its shell.

Intent on mating,
the male
pursues the
female to
subdue her.

Useful Addresses

California Turtle and
  Tortoise Club
P.O. Box 7300
Van Nuys, CA 91409

Desert Turtle Preserve
  Committee
P.O. Box 463
Ridgecrest, CA 93555

National Turtle and
  Tortoise Society
P.O. Box 66935
Phoenix, AZ 85082

The New York Turtle and
  Tortoise Society
163 Amsterdam Ave.,
  Ste. 465
New York, NY 10023

Other Resources

You can ask questions of
your pet store owner, as
well as the faculty of any
local university that offers
herpetology courses.

Literature

USEFUL BOOKS
Conant, Roger and Joseph
  T. Collins. *Reptiles and
  Amphibians, Eastern/
  Central North America.*
  Boston: Houghton Mif-
  flin, 1991.
Ernst, Carl H., et al. *Tur-
  tles of the United States
  and Canada.* Washing-
  ton, DC: Smithsonian
  Institution Press, 1994.
  and R. W. Barbour.
  Turtles of the World.
  Washington, DC:
  Smithsonian Institute
  Press, 1989.

USEFUL MAGAZINES
Reptile Hobbyist
One TFH Plaza
Neptune City, NJ 07753

Reptiles
P.O. Box 6050
Mission Viejo, CA 92690

Reptiles and Amphibians
  magazine
RD3, Box 3709-A
Pottsville, PA 17901

Published originally under the title *Die Schildkröte*

© 1997 by Gräfe und Unzer Verlag GmbH, München

English translation © Copyright 1998 by Barron's Educational Series, Inc.

All inquiries should be addressed to:
Barron's Educational Series, Inc.
250 Wireless Boulevard
Hauppauge, New York 11788

http://www.barronseduc.com

Library of Congress Catalog No. 98-4265

International Standard Book Number 0-7641-5117-7

Library of Congress Cataloging-in-Publication Data
Wilke, Hartmut, 1943–
    [Schildkrote. English]
    Turtles and tortoises : caring for them, feeding them, understanding them / Hartmut Wilke ; photography, Uwe Anders ; illustrations, Renate Holzner.
       p. cm. — (Family pet series)
    Includes bibliographical references and index.
    ISBN 0-7641-5117-7
    1. Turtles as pets. I. Title. II. Series: Family pet.
SF459.T8W5313   1998
639.3'92—dc21   98-4265
                         CIP

PRINTED IN HONG KONG
9 8 7 6 5 4 3 2 1

Acknowledgments

The author and the publisher wish to thank Reinhard Hahn for contributing the section on the law and the turtle owner and Dr. Renate Keil for the section on signs of illness, under "Preventive Care and Health Problems," on pages 78 through 85.

Important Note

The electrical equipment described in this book for use with terrariums and aquariums (pages 50–63 and pages 68–69) must be of UL-listed design and construction. Keep in mind the hazards associated with the use of such electrical appliances and wiring, especially near water.

The use of an electronic circuit breaker that will interrupt the flow of electricity if there is damage to appliances or wiring is strongly recommended.

A protective switch, which must be installed by an electrician, serves the same purpose.

About the Author

Dr. Hartmut Wilke studied marine biology and fisheries science at the Universities of Mainz and Hamburg, Germany. He did his doctoral research on diseases in fish. From 1973 to 1983, he was the director of the Exotarium at the Zoological Garden in Frankfurt am Main, Germany. Since 1983, he has been the director of the Vivarium Zoological Garden in Darmstadt, Germany.

About the Photographer

The photographs in this book were taken by Uwe Anders, except for those by Kahl (pages 42 and 43) and Reinhard (page 36, bottom photo, and page 42, top photo).

Uwe Anders has a degree in biology and has been active for many years as a freelance nature photographer and a cameraman for nature film productions. He writes articles on nature, and he lectures at various institutions about nature photography and travel photography. His photographs appear in several pet owner's guides published by Barron's Educational Series.

About the Artist

Renate Holzner works as a freelance illustrator in Regensburg, Germany. Her broad repertoire ranges from line drawings to photorealistic illustrations and computer graphics.

Box turtles are especially fond of worms.